SKIP AHOY !
THE JOURNEYS BEGIN

Chapter 1

   AS I climbed out of the taxi I was astounded by the noise on the dock . The Taxi driver said something ." What ! " . " Is he staying there " , nodding at my travel companion ." Er , no ", then a bit more confidently ," He's absolutely buggered". I leaned into the open taxi door , " C'mon Tony , we're at the dock " . "John , I must have nodded off " . He yawned and continued . "Has he said which ship it is" ," No ,but he's over there talking to that guy with the briefcase under his arm , oh hey up , he's coming over" . "Hi lads " , he introduced himself

,"I'm from Falmouth pool , we are just sorting out ships for you all , wont be long now "and with that rejoined his colleague , also from Falmouth pool who had travelled with us in the taxi . There had been a second taxi carrying three more ratings from the pool office and they came over and joined us with their kit . The know it all of the three piped in .
" I've shipped out of here before , they're not sticking me on an effin tub , if they try It I'll stick em one on ". "What was your last post" I inquired . "Table waiter on the Star line and I told them what they could do with their effin job " . I replied "I cant imagine why you left " ? ."
I think they had it in for me" he replied . I quipped "That must have hurt " . The rest chuckled but he went on , "It did " , More stifled laughter . " I told em , I can take it

". Riotous laughter ensued and our learned worldly wise friend was suspiciously confused. Were we laughing at him, or with him. He decided the latter and joined in the laughter. That made us howl even more. "Getting on lads". The guy with the briefcase and his colleague rejoined our party ",We've sorted it out. Grab your gear and follow us". The three, and Tony my companion from Goole pool were taken along the dockside towards their ship but the guy with the briefcase steered me towards a pontoon with small fishing boats lazily bobbing around. Stopping at one of them he said. "Get in the boat and I'll hand you your gear". It always surprises me how submissive to orders one can be but mechanically and without question, especially after two days of travelling and very little sleep , I followed his instructions. " The boatman's going to take you to your ship , Its the one anchored in the bay ". My eyes following the general direction of his pointing finger . "The orangey coloured one" I queried . "Er yes "he offered " . "Loose the aft line boy ", the boatman said and , complying , we left the pontoon . He pointing the bow in no general direction to the ship in the bay . "This your first trip boy ", he chirped hopefully wanting to start a life long friendship until we got to the ship . "Yeah ".My heart sank as I realized the ship wasn't orange , it was rust . We had been going about 5 minutes and I thought . We don't seem to be getting any closer , also the sea state was becoming increasingly rough ." Better hang on boy it's going to get rougher than this" . and he broke into a sea shanty about sinking which cheered me up no end . I've had a few regrets in my young life . Not getting my hands inside Liz Ravensfield's bra etc , but this boat ride was beginning to be a very close second . The ship , became a colossus against the tiny fishing boat as we arrived alongside and started riding and dropping some three feet due to the swell , " Where's the gangway "! I asked very disturbed by the inhospitable waters . There came a cry from up above . No , not the lord , someone on the ship . "Tie your kit on to this " . I looked up . Just in time , to get clobbered by a line that dangled a foot above the deck of the fishing boat , but in the next second was four feet In the air .This isn't going to be easy on a bouncing boat . I caught hold of the rope and managed to gain some slack , just enough to make it possible to tie my kit on , stood back and waved my arm to those atop . The guy on the other end of the line hauled , and all my worldly goods went heavenwards." But how am I ? ". Crack ! .A Jacob's ladder came rattling down the side of the ship . ,."Jump for it boy ", I looked at the fisherman in disbelief, "You've got to be fucking joking" . "Get on the ladder boy or you can swim back ". My lifelong friend what happened to my lifelong friend ? . I tried grabbing the ladder but realized with the swell I was going to have to go for it on the apex of the rise ." Now "! he shouted . I clung . Oh how I clung ,and then clung some more . This was madness . I was on the ladder and the friendly fisherman was away . I tried to step up but the ladder swung away from the ship which caused me to grip even tighter . Above , " Come on son , stop admiring the view ,we haven't got all day " . My response of effs and anything else I could think of was lost in the sound of the ship's engines vibrating through the plates . Coming to life , and I thought , we were moving forward . What the fuck .They're trying to kill me , then realised we were still riding the anchor . I thought .Right you bastards I'll show you . Anger and a will to kill erupted within my very being and I began to climb , but some eight feet still to climb I was spent and , looking down , I was truly considering a swift end when suddenly, the ladder began to move upwards. Renewal of life surged through my veins as I rose majestically from a certain watery grave .

I grabbed the guard rail and vaulted over onto the deck . I was faced with three deckhands laughing , responsible no doubt , but thankfully , for my meteoric rise . One of the deckhands quipped . "You shouldn't have tried that with your overcoat on " .I offered , "I always do things the hard way " . but then regretted saying it . "C'mon son , let's get you somewhere to bed down" ," your on duty tomorrow ". The aft accommodation consisted of a small galley . A dining come sitting area . A table garnished with books and magazines , Hmm nice tits , I'll have a butchers at that one later ." It'll be your job to keep this tidy lad . I'll explain the rest of your duties tomorrow morning " Be on deck for six a.m . Your in number six at the bottom of the companionway.

Evening meal is six on the dot, if your not there you go without". What is it about ultimatum speeches that give a person power over the lower classes, the lesser bred, the serfs. This was no ordinary individual, this was being announced by the boson of a shit tip ship.

He left the galley, down or up, who cares, I was still affected by my experience on the Jacob's and my sudden recollection caused me to jump for the kitchen sink where I unceremoniously dumped my breakfast, the first and last time I was sick at sea .. The adventure, the quest for discovery in the face of adversity was rapidly becoming, "What on earth have I done ".

Wearily, the energy, now spent from my already tired body. I rescued my gear and proceeded to negotiate the companion way down to my cabin ,Ah ! Here it is , number six . I looked around the small cabin . In one corner there seemed to be a tall steel box which later was identified to me as a wardrobe .The opposite side contained the bed which rested on four metal bars from the ceiling to the floor. That was it . No carpet no desk no drawers . Nothing . , Hmm , homely eh ! . On the bed there were clean folded sheets and a couple of laundered blankets that were showing signs of age . On making the bed I realised that my first observation was not keen enough and worn was definitely on the up . I checked the time with my watch . Quarter past one . I decided to relax , get out of my decent clothes and put on Jean's and casual shirt and climbed onto the bed .it was then I noticed the vibration of the ship's engine which seemed to increase in intensity within the solitude of the small room . Hope I will be able to sleep with that racket going on . I lit my last fag , took a huge inhale of smoke that made me splutter and cough . Oh heck , where am I going to put it out , no flipping ashtray . I recovered the discarded packet and nipped the lit end which fell into the foil wrapping in the empty packet . Resting my head on the pillow my mind meandered back to the start of this adventure .

Chapter 2
From the age of 12 I had worked in a cafe , washing the used pots during my school dinner break . One year later I also landed a paper round , I say paper round

it was 2 rounds in the morning and one in the evening , boosting my earnings substantially. I also worked on a farm on Sunday. I was a quid short of my dads salary . All told , I was doing just fine . The realisation that this would come to an end upon reaching the ripe old age of fifteen never entered my uneducated mind . When the time finally did come and I had to go and register for my National insurance number and this tax thing , whatever that is , I was confused about what I was entering into . Then . My first interview . Ha ! . BRW . A piped television company stringing cables all across my home town the city of Sheffield . I was led into the office by a young woman and introduced to the General Manager. . He started chattering on about the job ,rather boringly I thought .

This allowed me to let my mind meander, giving me a chance to think about my date the previous evening, Eileen Grazer and her ample breasts, when suddenly he said ,"Well what do you think"!"Wha! Er er". The picture of unbuttoning her blouse rapidly fading. "What does it pay", "Well for forty hours a week how does two pounds four shillings and ten pence sound". I waited, expecting a punchline to the joke but none came.. Is this guy taking the piss and sarcastically I said "Is that an hour". I thought he was going to fall out of his chair. "You what, Even I don't get that ". He looked at me suspiciously. I went on, "I don't understand wages yet ", blatant bloody liar you've been creaming it for the last three years. " So what happens next" I offered. "Well ", gathering himself together. "If I decide that you are suitable for the job . I mean , you're a little on the short side for carrying ladders " he let a chuckle cluck out of his lips , Well , give the man an apple for spotting the obvious. " But as I say If you come back tomorrow , same time , I will have made my mind up " . And upon that announcement he rose from the chair , offered his hand and I thought he was offering me the bus fare home .No such luck , he wants me to shake it , Ugh it was limp , like a wet dish cloth ,and he marched me to the door. It was like being released to breathe gods fresh air and I gulped ravenously at the opportunity vowing never , ever , to enter this God forsaken pit of carnal slave drivers ever again . TWO POUNDS , FOUR SHILLINGS AND FUCKING TENPENCE I retorted venomously . and repeated and repeated then . Why not a song ! . So singing my words to the music of " it's a long way to tipperary" it lifted my spirit for about thirty seconds then becoming tiresome . The walk home was ponderous . That evening after three enquiries from my family members as to . " How did you get on ". I began to think ." What am I going to do "? My Mother was charging board at one pound and ten shillings for my brother and one pound for my sister . If I parted with one pound ten shillings I would have fourteen shillings and ten pence . Even less as I would have to pay tax and national insurance . Then clothes and things . The remainder to last me for a week ?, Useless . Absolute daylight robbery . It was then the idea struck me , I will join the army ,no , better still the navy . They get paid well and board and lodgings for free . Cracked it , and jumped up and took the stairs to my bedroom two at a time , grabbed on arrival , my note pad and pen and …..then it struck home ". Eighteen . I had to be Eight flipping teen " . Think ? Aha , careers office nine o clock tomorrow morning . .It was a restless night.

The following morning saw me down at the careers office bright and early . Two queues started to form . No hoper's and no ideas . Well you've got to start somewhere! . It turned nine and that was the cue for the No Hoper's Male voice choir to break into grumbling , "Are yer opening today then or what" . Answered by the tenor section . "Its their coffee time , they've been here five minutes " . Chuckles flooded the faces of the faceless and in answer to their jibes the doors noisily swung open and we filed in . I headed directly for youth careers and upon entering was approached by a smartly dressed lady in her fifties . " Can I help you love" . I thought , Well , yes if you've a mind to then dismissed it just as quickly. "Er yes Miss ". her eyes brightened to the address ," I was thinking about a career in the navy but" , "You have to be eighteen for that ", she finished the sentence and the nod of my head pinned a full stop on it . She went on in thought and then said , "There's always the Merchant Navy ". Oh , a glimmer of a question rose to my lips but before I could ask it she continued "You know we import goods from all over the world in fact I think it's the biggest navy in the world " . Turning and asking a colleague the same, he confirmed. It was the biggest in the world.". " Just a minute ". She went across to a cupboard and thumbing through a few brochures exclaimed Aha!. Gripping the brochure and clear delight on her face this elegant old lady seemed twenty years younger. What a smile can do. She sidled up to me and opened the brochure, I tried stepping around her to stand alongside her but she turned some more so I was forced to stand looking over her shoulder at the brochure together."Quite a feat at five foot two inches. "This is one of their training ships. The Vindicatrix " she began. "You have to go there to train for the type of job ". She prattled on positively oblivious of my presence, it was her day of celestial being. I was having difficulty keeping up with her enthusiasm and my thoughts were racing and I wanted to sit down with that brochure and read it at my speed . I would have had to wrestle her to the ground to get her to release that bloody brochure but tried , " Can I have a look "? . " Yes certainly " . and she put her body even closer into me , offering up the page she was reading . " No I mean can I take it away " . "Oh no it's the only copy we have got" . "Well could I read it or take an address to write to ". " Oh , I do all of that dear ! Come over to my desk and we can discuss it ". The lamb followed . Hmm , she's not in bad shape . A woman's backside always fascinates me . We arrived at her desk and me wishing she was leaning back against me once more .Testosterone plus fifteen years old equals chaos ! . We talked and her enthusiasm was magnetic and all to soon I was committed to . "A life on the ocean waves" . Her statement not mine . A couple of phone calls later and she was now in full flight piecing together the necessary documents required to go forward , and I , having no other options but two pounds , four shillings and ten pence , allowed myself to be manipulated into this career . The Merchant Navy . A Merchant Seaman , This Happy Breed set in a silver sea etc . When I came out of the building thanking her kindly for escorting me down the steps to the open doorway , I was hooked on the idea and very surprised that she didn't offer to write ! . I owe that dear sweet lady everything , as to what followed , shaped the boy into the character of the man I could live with . Time passes like lightening and time creeps along like a shuffling old man but always adverse to your urgency , until at last , the day came for me to catch the train to Sharpness Training School for Merchant seamen , . My mother bless her . My faithful companion who had mopped many a tear from my eye whilst growing up , came to the railway station to see me on my way . As we waited on the platform together she talked aimlessly about things that had passed and I took her in my arms and gave her a hug . As she rested there a sob or two reluctantly emmitted and she drew away saying , " There , that's enough of that . Now don't forget you change trains at Birmingham" , she collected her fortitudinal armour . " No mum and thanks for everything ", again a stifled sob from her . A sound like thunder erupted and echoed through the metal roofing of the station announcing the arrival of my steel steed . Its awareness causing the hairs on the back of my neck to stand on end . I grabbed my suitcase and entered the nearest carriage door which slammed shut behind me . My mother on one side of the door on the platform mouthed , "Goodbye love look after yourself" whilst I tried in vain to release the window strap on the door to no avail . The train began to move and I shouted ." Bye mam ". Rapturous chuckles ensued . I turned toward the sounds and realized it was an open carriage and a dozen or more faces had witnessed the parting of mother and son . I felt the rush of blood to my face . Lifting the heavy suitcase I sheepishly walked down the carriage past the smiling faces, looking for a seat. Ah, there's one. I tried to lift the suitcase up onto the luggage rack but my strength failed me on my first attempt, then on my second attempt I just missed a blokes head which caused even more chuckles but the suitcase landed with an almighty thump on the rack. I collapsed into the seat and when the chuckles finally died down I then plucked up courage to look around at the fellow travellers. Nonchalantly of course. Mixed bunch . Couple of servicemen their uniforms identifying them. Hmm, twelve weeks and I'll have a uniform too.

Chapter 3

The sound of raised voices outside the cabin door brought me back to the present, I instinctively jumped up from the bed . I could here voices that were competing to be heard , should I put my head out , no , most likely get it pushed back in judging the anger in the voices . Then recognising that familiar voice of authority, The boson , quietening the situation between the two. A thump thump on the door of my cabin followed by , " C'mon boy it's teatime " . I must have been asleep but didn't dwell on the thought for long as I was reminiscent of the fact . "If your not there at six you'll go without ". I took the companionway steps two at a time much to the amusement of the deckhands sauntering towards them . "Somebody's in a hurry " . Yes mate , I thought . I am . In fact I'm starving having surrendered breakfast . Into the kitchen , grabbed a plate from the hotplate and put it down twice as fast . Ran over to the sink and cooled the reddened fingers underneath the cold running water tap . "Now that'll teach yer son to wait your turn" , the boson piped in . " These lads have been working all day ". So that's why they were all stood back and I fell for it . "Come on lad sit down here " . One of the older hands gestured an empty chair . Instinctively I felt at the chair ,I didn't want to slip up a second time , no that's ok . "So lad where are you from " . " I'm" ," Is this your first trip " ." Er yes , I'm from " .. Where did you do your training" , " Sheffield." ." Yer did yer training at Sheffield? " . " No . I'm from Sheffield I did my training at Sharpness " . "Ah . Old Vindi " another one piped . Did you tit the figurehead " .some of the others laughed but the guy went on . " It's TRUE. You had to crawl out along the bowsprit , only a few lads ever do it " . My confirmation of being one of the elite was met by applause and good lad . The meal jogged along with light banter and I was beginning to enjoy the atmosphere . Those who had finished eating putting their plates in the sink and walking away . Walking away , oh heck I bet I have to wash up . Now here's something I can show them how to do . Three years before the sink and all that . Within six minutes I had washed and dried every plate and fighting iron they had used . I received nods of approval and a welcoming comment , "He's going to be alright ". I meandered over to the settees , not to sit down but to try and sneak a peep at the magazine I had noticed earlier but a big nasty looking character who would have easily made blackbeards knees knock had beaten me to it . I later found out there was a pecking order for these treats and a quick calculation confirmed to me that my turn would come on my eighty first birthday , given that the pages were not stuck together by that time . So with nothing else to do I meandered on deck and was welcomed by the intoxicating atmosphere of a fresh sea breeze . Home , set in a silver sea . What was that damn poem . " Hello there" , a friendly voice called . I turned to see an elderly chap but very smartly rigged . He went on ," You must be the new chap " ,and offered his hand . "We all had a laugh at your expense on the ladder he he " . " Yeh it wasn't my finest hour Sir", then , "Are you the captain" . " No I'm the chief engineer, you'll have to learn quite quickly if your going to make it

". " Have you been with the ship a long time" I enquired . "Five , no six years . She doesn't 't look much now but if you want to see the world this is the ship to do it with" . That encouraged me to a degree that at least I wont be pottering around the coast ." Ah well I'd best get below nice speaking to you lad " and he bade me goodnight . So , blue water all the way , but where ? Nobody had said and foolishly, I hadn't asked . I had toured the ship twice and as the light was starting to fade I made my way to my cabin . On arrival I lit the remainder of my last fag . Sank back onto the pillow and strangely started to think of where I had left off .

Chapter 4

" Birmingham ", the guard announced, Birmingham , the train slowed to a stop . I reached up and retrieved my suitcase and made for the awkward door that I had trouble with earlier . Stepping out onto the station platform , I immediately went to enquire from the nearest station guard as to my connecting train to Sharpness . " Platform three lad . Leaves in fifteen minutes" . Then proffered ," that's it on the end ". Thankyou . On reaching the train he had indicated I again asked a second guard , and again confirmation was given . The journey became very tedious as the train driver insisted on stopping at every station and every time it stopped , I was double checking the platform name . This went on and on for what seemed a lifetime . At one station there seemed to be quite a commotion from the lower carriages . The slamming and opening of carriage doors accompanied by someone shouting grew nearer and then this character appeared in uniform , "Sharpness sea training school" . I had never moved so fast and I was on that platform like greased lightning . There was roughly fifty or sixty youths all came piling out of the train like sacrificial lemmings and milling around on this tiny platform . The uniformed man joined us . Blew his whistle and commanded "All of you follow me ". Off he went at a gait that would have made third place in the Olympics and us scurrying along carrying our suitcases , After what seemed a mile the line of hopefuls began to wain and wallow . Bodies were all over the place as the suitcases we were carrying became leadened and unmanageable. We finally arrived at the gates to a multitudinal moaning from the ones who still had the strength to breathe . "Right ". The whistle blower shouted . "I'm taking you down to your billets " . Outside the barrack rooms we formed two lines . Catering and deckhands . Whistle blower continued ," Right when I blow my whistle ," I want you all to go into your billet huts , pick a bunk and put your coats into your lockers and then come back out here , understood. Fast as you can" and blow he did . No sooner were we in and complying when he came into the hut ,"Outside , get outside now . Go outside . Leave your coats" . Everyone complied and filed outside and we waited . And then waited , waited some more ," What's he doing in there" someone offered . Two of the deckhand recruits after a few suspicions comments from our group drummed up the courage to walk back into the barracks where they found whistle blower going through each locker , helping himself to the contents of peoples jacket pockets . On confronting him with the theft he started to yell "Outside , Outside "but these two having witnessed his deeds took hold of him either side and marching him outside and declared his actions to the lot of us . "Hang the bastard "seemed a bit harsh to my reckoning but the threats were multitudinous . The guy was escorted to the main office whereupon he was later arrested by the police and we never clapped eyes on him again . Nor for that matter the money he had stolen from us which , I could never work out the reason of the non return . What a day , we all looked like starved rats , like something out of Oliver Twist . Well at least whistle blower Fagin will be in jail feeling the same as us . There was a bit of bravado banter going on between the lads but soon became subdued due to the long day we had endured . Some of the Scots lads had been travelling sixteen hours , poor buggers. The guy on the bunk below popped his head out looked up and said ", Hi , Where are you from" . "Sheffield " .I replied , " Not far from me then , I'm from Hull", he continued "my name is John ". . " Well I wont forget that in a hurry" . " Oh" he enquired , " Why's that then "? . " Because they call me John , get it , that's why I wont forget it" . "Oh yeah I see ", but he didn't sound or look convinced . Then started to say, "Do you think we ". but was interrupted by a bloke in uniform shouting . " Supper time lads line up outside . Make sure your lockers are locked we've had enough thieving for one day ". The offer of food . Well you can imagine the stampede , people were losing their shoes and then being trampled on when they tried to retrieve them which caused more to trip and fall . But once outside the line up could not have been bettered by the Queens guards performing trooping of the colour . Even the uniform commented ," Have you been practicing" which brought forth a cheery half-hearted laugh . "Right lads right turn let's go" . At first I thought some of the lads had changed their minds about going but then realizing not everyone knows their right from their left , they sheepishly rejoined the rest of us who were tittering , tittering now theirs an interesting subject but food was more appealing . The line of hopefuls knowing that food was at hand and willing to be devoured didn't waver or linger in fact the pace started picking up to a degree that Uniform , determined to lead the five thousand to the five loaves and two fishes , started to run to keep in front , whereupon the multitude seeing his enthusiasm to be the first to arrive began to chase after him and the sound of boots on soil it suddenly became the five thirty at Cheltenham . Flushed , we arrived alongside and stood in awe of Vindicatrix . A tea clipper from the past , her line was majestic , one of the fastest ships of her time ,sat in a lock , what a waste." Right lads" puffed uniform , "follow me on board" then added, " No rushing ". And comply we did, to a man. The saloon was on the second deck so we all enjoyed sliding down the companion bars. The first thing I noticed was how low the deck roof was, and all timber. We took a seat as requested by our mentor who then explained the rules of engagement with the galley staff. "Right, single file lads ". he walked toward a shuttered counter that opened to his presence. Three motley servers started handing to each of us a pint mug of piping hot scouse (a thick vegetable meaty type of soup), the next server gave out a lump of bread which if you had dropped it on your foot , would have left you limping for a week . We returned to the table rather pleased with our trophies. Banter subdued ,chatter sparse, but munching and slurping invigoratingly rapturous . Ah , now this is what we signed up for , the finer things in life , quaffing copiously , quality confirmed , the end to what I can only describe as an interesting first day .

I was awoken abruptly the following morning by the leader of the billet , a position usually awarded to a toughie to control the rest of the cadets and saved on employing a steward . He seemed to revel in whacking the pick axe handle which he carried , on the iron bunk rails shouting at the top of his voice " Get up you idle effers get your wash kits and towels , its ablutions for you stinkers" . He had employed a similar kind of attitude the previous night upon our return from supper . Threats of violence if we didn't settle down for sleep ,double quick , had rattled one of the Scottish lads who offered to accommodate this bullying tactic . I think it was to be reconvened by the two at a later more agreeable meeting place . There is something about cold water at six in the morning that for some , never bodes well , and now , stood at the row of sinks , faced with both prospects a number of the lads I could see were rather reluctant to enjoy the experience . Myself on the other hand had grown up with these tasty delights and I dove into the refreshing waters with much gusto and vocal approval . It was this darn shaving I couldn't get used to and this was the morning of the third attempt in my short lifetime to get it right . Now gently I told myself , don't drag the blade , plenty of soap . Well , that didn't go so bad said I as I stuck the bits of toilet paper over a dozen cuts or so . Getting quite professional now ! . The promise of breakfast soon made me forget this minor setback to the blood banks loss of doubling its quota and looking like I had been stood too close to an attack with a sticky newspaper I disregarded the titters from my shipmates and filled an expectant belly . I was so hungry they could have fed us any crap , It was only later the quality of the meal was questioned in that context . One or two were lucky enough to survive the treatment given in the sick bay but the rest of our group formed a reluctant sit in vigil at the camp toilet block . Ah the fun of it all . This is the life , and thoughts of Scotland as we piped ourselves aboard a toilet seat ensued by the remains of our breakfast . We were later that day introduced to our course tutor . A reluctant fellow to smile but very professional in his approach he explained things forwards backwards and sideways to the point where even the slowest fully grasped the gist of the lesson . Knots came next , a firm favourite of mine in which I revelled in promoting my expertise by tying the requested bowline behind my back . This was short lived when he produced the same result but using only one hand . I had been dealt my first lesson , Learn your adversaries strengths and weaknesses. . We were given books on seamanship and instructed to learn the named points of a ship ." Learn them tonight and I'll test you in the morning ". "Now because you all had the trots this morning you should have collected your uniform so I will hand you over to Peter here to take you along to the storeroom ". "Thank you sir " Peter bade the retreating instructor. "Right lads if you would like to follow me ". Off we trailed yet again , yet nobody seemed particularly enthusiastic about receiving their uniforms but one thing I did notice , the introductory tactics by the instructors were beginning , very quickly ,to weld this motley crew of individuals into crewmates . Thirty six hours had passed since first walking through the camp gates . Only eleven weeks five and a half days left to go and we'd be shipping out ! . The next few weeks were pretty much the same, classroom then practical , classroom then practical but the difference in us from the boys who had entered this world of the sea was night to day . The school were rather strict on hair styles, or rather, the length. To maintain a degree of smartness they employed a character called Percy who revelled in his position as the camp barber. I use the word camp as to his nature as touching up determined the quality of the haircut received. Boldness meant baldness. "Hey lads guess what"., a student of the royal art of seamanship came running in, " There's going to be a boxing tournament between us and Gravesend sea school ". he announced excitedly ." We have to pick someone from our billet to represent us. we have to wait to see which weight category is available for our billet". Please, let it be heavyweight. I shuddered at the prospect of stepping into a ring. I had studied judo for two years, the gentle art of self defence at our local youth club

. Pugilism was not me at all . But others were chattering on excitedly over the prospect of defending the billets honour to the death ,and , if need be even worse ! . Two days later same man same bad news "Its featherweight " he announced pretending that he was disappointed because it didn't fall in his weight class . I became increasingly aware of being stared at , and , looking up confirmed my uneasiness . "What weight are you John" ? . "You can eff off if you think I'm climbing into a boxing ring" . "No seriously what weight are you" . "How heavy is featherweight" ? . "About nine and a half to ten stone . "Well that's half the lads in here so don't look at me " . I was agitated by their inference that I was to be the patsy and welcomed John from Hull entering the billet and upon hearing the fight weight stating, " He's mine "." I used to box at the club" he went on, and on, and, on some more and I felt a bit uneasy because when somebody doesn't come up for air, they end their prattle by saying things like. "But the doctor after the last fight I had, said it would be dangerous to fight ever again ". or some excuse like that. The day of the visit arrived. We greeted the Gravesend lot with the usual good mannered wolf whistles, gybes and any other insult that came to mind ." Look at her with the handbag "was a classic which resulted in laughter giving a short reprieve of insults to our guests. Oh well, if we get clobbered now. We asked for it. And did we get it. Four fights down and Sharpness were going well and truly out . But surely salvation was going to come in the form of John from Hull , but where the effin hell was he ? And it's the next fight ! . The weed from Gravesend who climbed in the ring although tallish looked like you could blow him over he was so skinny ." Has anybody seen John" ? the billet controller asked . "No no " came the replies ." Right Yorkie you're going in " . No fucking no came my reply ." Look " . the billet batterer went on , "either you go in there or I give you a thumping and it'll be a lot worse than he can dish out , look at him you could blow him over ". " Is everybody at Sharpness afraid to face this lad " , the master of ceremonies announced ". We're just getting him ready" replied the billet batterer , "come on Yorkie the master of ceremonies is waiting" . "Master of ceremonies, does he do funerals" I chirped . Crikey what's happened to my voice ".I want to go to the loo" . Where the effin hell is John from Hull . Too late ! Too late ! , they had me in shorts but had to take off one of the gloves as in their rush they had forgotten to remove the shirt sleeve from my arm . Anybody , No , I mean Any person who has walked up to a boxing ring for the first time , it's cold, and you feel tired , so tired your limbs are like lead , your cheeks go cold and your mouth feels like you've swallowed the Sahara desert . But the cheers , don't they lift you ? That's right , they fucking don't . I had to be helped up the steps and into the ring . Well , forced then ! . Its lonely , everybody's out there and yet your isolated . "Right lad" the corner man said , "Pop this gum shield in and go to the centre of the ring ". A new cheer from somewhere which caused me to look back at my corner hoping that John from Hull had shown up Yes ! , *No* . "Right lad "said master of ceremonies " what took you so long , what's your name lad ". With a gum shield its impossible but I tried . "Its Bob representing Sharpness against " . I again tried saying John , "Oh sorry its Rod " . Oh what the fuck , get on with it I uttered under my quickening breath . "Against Alan from Gravesend , give a big cheer everybody." The reprieved obeyed . "Right I'll hand you over to the referee". "Right lads , try and keep it clean . I will not allow either one of you to get hurt so if you've had enough let me know and I'll stop the fight. Best of luck to you both , shake hands go to your corners and come out fighting" . I was going to enquire, "How soon can you ask" but my fists in the gloves got clobbered by the thing I was supposed to blow over , and , it hurt . Ding , and then fucking dong . I turned to find a maniacal opponent who seemed to have grown extra arms and under a rain of punches and shoves I sank to the canvas . Alongside the ring came billet batterer screaming "Get up or I'll kill you " . Well , why didn't you ask nicely last time ". I was shaking and I seemed to be in a cold sweat . But was back on my feet at five by the kindly considerate and thoughtful alternative I had been given . The ref said "Are you ok" and I made the mistake of nodding my head .and his words" Right box on" drowned out my ,"When can I pack in ". But I was back into it , However this time he charged into an empty corner with his arms flailing all over the place . I had ducked away just in time to avoid his attack and I caught him with a solid right on the back of the neck . Boo's abound came from a distant planet and as he turned he swung at my retreating body and hit me full in the nose . I suddenly felt sick and cold and wanted to go home . "You ok son" the ref said . "I ", but he must have thought I was Scottish and had said aye ! . "Box on " . I moved to the centre of the ring and the octopus I had been facing was suddenly down to two hands and for some reason standing off . I tried a jab , then another and there was no response . Has his corner asked him to slow down . Wallop , on my fucking nose again , but this time it stung like crazy . I tried a swinging right which he easily dodged by some six feet and he suddenly came running at me .

Two years of judo practice and being considered quite good kicked in and as he swung, I stuck my foot onto his ankle caught his arm in mine and twisted sideways helped by a very mild right to his face and down he went. A perfect Tsuri comi goshi. Ankle throw to the layman. But innocent enough to assume he had fallen over in his charge and I had caught him with a punch. The room could have been Wembley stadium as the cadets screamed for joy. "Yorkie Yorkie ". The guy was complaining to the ref but seemed more concerned over his wrist. The ref took him to his corner to have it examined whereupon they gave him the thumbs down. A quick chat from the ref brought back into the ring the Master of ceremonies who announced. "Due to Alan being unable to continue , we declare Rod the winner by a technical knockout ". " Rod Rod we want Rod " . Its fucking John , at last being able to spit out the gum shield , and then I thought leave it . I can always prove I am John if anyone comes looking . If you know what I mean . They carried me from the ring probably two yards then dropped me as the Master of ceremonies announced" Everyone down to Vindicatrix for supper " . I was sat on my own , tugging with my teeth at the laces to the gloves and managed to free a hand and I suddenly felt empty and no , not empty , ashamed , I felt ashamed .and crying within , and fought more convincingly than I had in the ring , to withhold the tears . I came to terms with myself later by realizing he was out to hurt me whereas I was only wanting to save myself .

Chapter 5

I felt a hand on my shoulder. "C'mon lad". I'm not going for supper ". A laugh , then a more determined" Cmon lad its quarter to six ". I sat bolt upright in the bunk . Oh heck ! The retreating alarm said . "Keep the noise down lad , there's people been on night watch ". I swiftly dressed . A quick polish of the teeth with a dry brush and hey presto . I meandered onto the deck to be eyed questioningly by a rather annoyed man in the form of the boson . "What time do you call this" he said . I wanted to say . What everyone else calls it , six o clock ." Sorry I kinda laid in" . "Have you done the dishes from the four o clock shift change ". He knew the answer , "have you tidied the sink in the kitchen and rest room ? Have you cleaned the washroom sinks and the toilets ?. Look lad , I expect you to think about these things as second nature . It's good news for you that the lads have pitched in and done it for you but try and earn their respect by having it done , alright " . A nod sufficed as I was so deflated by his attack . "At sea school ", he went on , "they give you the skeleton of the job . Then when you come on a ship we put the organs , the sinew and the meat and form a man capable of helping his crewmates in good times and in times that are not so good ". He seemed to dwell on his last statement with remorse which I found out later to be his experience of being torpedoed during the war and in a lifeboat for sixteen days . Having to eat the flesh of a comrade who had died from injuries sustained from burning oil . "Right let's get to your duties " . I followed him to the lifeboat deck . "First the blocks on the davits of the lifeboats" ." I want them greased , also the davit spindles blocks and winches" ." I want you to take this pad and pencil and make a full list of everything in the lifeboat lockers including the dates on the food and especially the flares . I also want the water changing ok" . "Yes boson ". " I'll be back in five minutes to check you've done it all" , then laughed ,"No , only kidding son "and off he went . Right ,I thought . Make amends for this morning I told myself and I got stuck into the tasks at hand . Some three hours later he showed up ." Come on lad , your missing your tea , How's it going " he enquired ." I've finished ". I stated rather proudly

,and handed him the inventory sheets ," , "and I have put a separate sheet for everything out of date" . "Have you done just this boat "? . "I've done all four ", I was beside myself in being able to see the wonderment on his face . "That's brilliant John , come and get some tea and some toast ". "I'm just going up to see the first mate , you get along and get your tea" . I walked into that kitchen like I owned it . Then seeing the pile of dirty cups and plates . Looking around seeing fag ash all over the place , dregs of tea spilt and came back down to earth with a bump . Some two hours later . Shift change and , everything that I had washed and cleaned was back in the sink . "Haven't you started washing those up yet "? , the bosons head appeared round the doorway ." I have but they've just been and used them all again" I offered limply. "Well come and find me when you've done ". Out on deck the ship was feeling alive . You could almost feel the joy of the motion of the sea cradling our steel home and it , excitedly responding to the caress of the waves . Sheer joy ! . "Finished bosun "., "Good lad , come with me . The first mate wants to meet you" ." I'm not smartly dressed" I protested . "You don't have to be in uniform lad ha ha ". Nervously I entered the superstructure of the ship , past the saloon and pantry kitchen . Turned right and confronted a door upon which the bosun wrapped his weathered knuckles . "Come in ". I was taken aback by the size of the accommodation . Stood before me , an officer in whites , some fifty years old or so . Well built , I later found out that he had played rugby . "Ah , so this is our new lad" , then , "no son , don't sit down you've got work to do . You made a very good job of the lifeboats and the bosons quite pleased with you so far . Its your first time at sea is it , you'll find it different to civvy street, well I just wanted to say keep up the good work and everything will work out fine . Right , on your way lad and thank you boson ". Outside on deck I said to boson , "He doesn't give you time to answer ". The boson grinned , then seriously, " He's the first mate lad . Next to the captain hes the man who has your welfare and mine in the palm of his hand and every praise that he gives you , he will double it in punishment for any misdemeanour . Right . go and join the lads up front , I'm going atop to the bridge" . Sauntering up to the bow I was greeted by the deckies , "Hey John yer alright mate . Hows yer finding it".. "Not bad "I replied ",bit different to sea school ". They laughed , "we've all been through that experience. Where are you from" . " From She "," Got any family in the merchant" . "effield " . No" . " Where are you from"?. , "Sheffield" I finally completed the name without interruption ." You'll be alright once you've settled in . Why don't you go and put the tea urn on and we'll be along in a minute for a brew ". I thought , how many cups of tea do you need but said Ok . I retired from the awkwardness of being an outsider feeling not wanted or trusted . Not yet . Back in the aft galley I had an idea . I would make a list of all the crew members names , preference tea or coffee sugar milk and allow them to fill in their appropriate details . I would stick it on the canteen wall . Then I could have the drinks ready for them rather than them losing ten minutes of their break time waiting around to make their own . Well , you'd have thought I had scored a goal for England against West Germany . Pat's on the back ." Well done son" ," It's a pity no one had the brains to think of it before ". I had cracked the ice . Even big nasty bugger allowed himself a grunt . He's beat me to that magazine again , I thought to myself . One of the deckies seeing my interest in the magazine instinctively knew what I was thinking said ." Forget it son , we've been waiting over a month to get our hands on it , he doesn't share anything . One dark night he'll find himself over the side ". I looked at him but said nothing but added a very knowing nod ." Were going to pick up a load of logs from Africa" announced the boson entering the canteen . "Africa ", one or two retorted . "Yes" he went on "West coast , Libreville I think . Were putting into Los Palmas in a couple of days to refuel . John I'll want you to see this done so if you can ask the other lads what it involves" . "Right bosun ". "Africa" ! , Said Mike when the boson had gone . "Oh were going to be alright there , all those lovely bronze bodies ". "I've been before , on the Trippet it was " . "Never got off the bloody ship . Anchored out and they bring the logs alongside in tiers". (Meaning a long line of logs all tied together width ways , like a floating ramp or bridge) . "Well I'll get ashore even if I have to swim" , Pete offered . "No matey" the experienced one continued ."You'd be dinner for the sharks . By instinct , they come circling when there's only a few logs left and the lad doing the slinging , if he slips in ". He left it there but everyone got the message . That night in my cabin I lay on my bunk staring at the ceiling . Africa , I had seen one or two movies starring Johnny Weissmuller . It'll have all altered now I consoled myself . Stifling a desiring urge to do a Tarzan scream . My mind drifted back .

Chapter 6
"Where have you been ", the billet toughie said ." We've all been worried about you . Why didn't you come down for supper ". I looked at this person despising his very being . Is he blind I thought and lifted my head to allow

greater light to fall on my bruised face but offered . " I've been to the sick bay ". "Have they said everything's alright ". asked but couldn't give a shit . "Something about cartledge damage" I half heartedly replied . I couldn't give a shit either . The rest of the billet was in darkness but on hearing my reply , I received . Well done John's and well done Yorkie's as I made my way to my bunk but no real emphatic congratulations . And , to be honest I didn't give a shit . "Well done John ".,came a voice from Hull but I ignored it with the contempt I thought it deserved . Later when I came to terms with my experience of the night , I realised I had been wrong to blame him for not being there . It's not a crime to be afraid , and we had both dealt with it in our own way . Oh , that dear sweet little old lady from careers , you've changed me .

Chapter 7

The purple mounds sat on the horizon on the dawn of the day were met with "The Canary islands "shouted Pete . I swiftly finished my clean up duty and went on deck and met a rush of deckies all making their way to the guardrail to get a glimpse of the spectacle . I considered this strange because they must have seen landfall many times before . It was only through time I realized the significance of this need . Freedom to not be contained by rules , to drink abundantly , meet ladies and yes , meet ladies . Avoid the dock rats tonight when you go ashore Pete was prattling on ," They give you more than you bargained for ".But everyone was aware of dock rats . Pete . "I wouldn't touch one even if she paid Me "! . That brought a laugh but the banter of our group was broken by ."Come on now lads you've all seen landfall before , get on with your jobs and make sure your hawsers are free of entanglements" . Gosh that boson he's a real slave driver . We went about our duties giving the odd glance toward the ever increasing size of the island and the purple changing to yellow sands and white buildings . We had come into Los Palmas along a channel that ran adjacent to the beach which had one small detached villa on it . Twenty years later when I returned to a skyscraper jungle . I just couldn't believe it . Coming in to port I was put in the bow gang . These lads were on the ball and we made fast , rigged the gantry for intake of fuel and were chomping at the bit to get ashore . "Ok" said boson . "I want volunteers for staying aboard ". Chins hit the deck .I wanted to be the first ashore but said ,"I'll make one of the volunteers", I couldn't believe I had said it , and then , regretted it . "Thanks John , who else , don't make me have to pick you ". " I'll keep the lad company" Reg said then went on ," I've seen it all before , andalucian anyway . Who wants to get the clap ".   . " Meee! " the crew shouted in unison and everybody laughed .

All, barring the idiots who volunteered , trooped ashore that night laughing and joking and here . Here's me . On deck . Never been to a foreign country in my life , stuck , on deck . We finished refuelling and Reg , Dave and myself along with

Three O , short for third engineer dismantled our temporary rig for the fuel line . Right , may as well go and make a brew I offered . "You'll have to bring it back on deck John "said Reg . "We cant leave the ship unattended" . Don't want any waifs and strays meandering onto the wrong ship . I thought to myself, I don't think anybody seeing this rust bucket would be caught dead on it . Then I chastised myself, it's not so bad . Early hours of the morning just when you could fall asleep on a washing line we became aware of the return of the toreadors . Olay's by the dozen pealing out . The staggering , 40 degrees to the left and then 40 degrees to the right and back four steps for good measure , and , to get their bearings for the final all out charge for the gangway . The carriers and the carried staggered up the gangway and onto the deck. Why they always think its necessary to put you in a bear hug, and then whisper. "Watch out for any drunks coming aboard". Not just one person, but six times is beyond me, then saying. "We don't want them spewing all over the ship". Thank fuck the other two were out on their feet but I regretted thinking that later The officer of the watch approached and said to me." Any one drunk Parkin "to which the obvious answer is " No Sir "!." Good, carry on then ". and disappeared back to his cabin and his bottle of whisky. Reg got the same treatment as me but being used to it seemed to break their clutches more easily. "Experience, either you've got it or you haven't" he prattled then more seriously. "Don't go down aft yet John.

Let them get settled otherwise they will have you making coffees teas sandwiches and it'll be six in the morning and that's the time we're on the tide ". An hour later I was relieved of gangway duty and told ," go and get yer head down lad" . Going aft I thought , I'll have a quick cuppa stepped into the aft galley and what met me nearly made me vomit . There was two broken mugs the contents being spilled on the floor , piles of sick where at least three had contributed to the cause , half drunk mugs abound , How can six grown men do this ! Then a thought of horror , what about the two carried aboard . I was going to go down to the toilet block to find out but the companion way was an evident copy of the galley . I retreated back into the galley to start mopping up operations when the boson appeared ," Why aren't you in bed Lad" the word freezing on his lips as he stared at the carnage . "Oh no ! I'm not having this on my ship ". I assured him I would clean up and thanking me he consoled himself by saying , "Well , I'll get no sense out of them tonight but wait while tomorrow morning" he said threateningly and thanked me for starting the clean up . I had just picked up the broken pieces of mugs when he reappeared. " You'd better come and have a look in the toilet block" . I followed him into our ablutions area and No ! Oh no ! . One of the passed out deckies had been left on the toilet but had been sick and then fallen forward onto his face and was lying in his own fecies . The sinks were full . We got the senseless deckie cleaned up and put him in his bunk . The boson said that he must be ready for the morning , excused himself ,p and turned in for what was left of the night . I set to , cleaning first the companionway , then the washroom and toilets , and finally the kitchen . Four thirty on the dot in walks the boson followed by four of the deckies . "Oh thank goodness , your up are you ". I could have knocked him out ," I haven't ben to bed , I've just this minute finished" . "Have you! . Well done . Nip down to your cabin and get something warm on and come with me . Were going to form a skeleton crew for departure so you need to be on your toes ". I joined him up front and was really surprised by the cool morning breeze coming over the bow ." Right John you Neil and me are one team . Reg ,Bill and Bob are aft , follow every thing I say and we'll be fine ". We released the tension at command from the bridge , caste off brought the hawsers in under steam and it went perfect . Receiving a pat on the back accompanied by a verbal ," I'm proud of you lad !" . I remained at the bow , feeling nine feet tall . The breeze grew stronger over the bow with the movement into open waters but right this minute was the greatest rush of satisfaction I had encountered since joining the ship . I had been on duty twenty six hours and it was now taking its toll on my stamina . The boson , once we were out of the channel and in clear water said , "Right John , get yourself along to your cabin , if anybody asks you to make them a tea just say the boson wants to see them . Now go and get your head down" . "Right boson ". At last my bunk , this jewel set in a silver sea

. I cant remember anything from my head touching the pillow and slept the sleep of the innocent for twelve hours solid only to be awakened by . "Have you died ". Came a voice at the cabin door ." I'm just catching up".,my reply . "Well consider yourself caught . On deck in fifteen minutes , your on the eight while twelve on the bridge ". Wow ! This is it . Everything I had been waiting for, at last , they realize the ship cant run without me . I was there in ten taking the companion steps to the bridge two at a time . Walked onto the bridge and said . "Reporting for duty Sir". The mate looked at me and said . "Glad you could join us ", then , "Right I've got a very important job for you to do" . Well , my mind was racing , lookout , helmsman , oh please let me steer the ship , I wont hit anything , plotting the course for Africa ? "I want you to take these mugs and I'll have tea two sugars and no milk . And the helmsman will have coffee no sugar no milk . Quick as you can , there's a good lad" . Dejected . Did I here somebody say dejected, two mugs handed to one mug . Well you can shove the bridge right up yer arse. Then changed my mind just in case he changed his mind as well . Tea with milk no sugar and coffee with sugar no milk er ! Sugar in the milk with coffee but no tea in the ,oh dear . I trooped back to the bridge . "That was quick , well done lad ". " Er , sorry sir , what did you ask for" . He re explained , rather nicely I thought , only using four letter words where it was deemed to be absolutely necessary ." Right sir I've got it now ". " You will get it ". was the last receding word I heard as I exited from the bridge at breakneck pace. There's a time for forgiving and a time for rekindling friendships thus upon presenting the steaming luxuries I received ." Right . get off the bridge and go and clean the ablutions , I don't want to see you for the rest of the watch ". Dejectedly, most deflatedly , absolutely disparagingly I muttered This is the life ! , is it ? It is is it ? So then it definitely is is it . And off I went . My sceptre in the form of a loo brush in one hand My challis a mop bucket in the other, ready to put the ship to right . For Queen and country . Well you've got to start somewhere, Hmm now let me see , how's about the crew ablutions then ! And for the second time in seventeen hours I was cleaning yet again .The clock meandered round rather slowly to eleven . Back in the rest room I looked for the elusive magazine but knew big nasty bugger would have it . I decided to make a repeat drink for the pair on the bridge . This time it was a more welcoming, " Thanks lad , just the job . Look go and get yourself tucked in" . I replied " Thanks Sir " and felt the retreat to my cabin was a reward in kind . But I would have given anything to have steered the ship . Maybe next time and closed my eyes , surrendering the day . The time on board a boat whilst at sea is , in general ,relaxing . Keeping things tidy and shipshape . You enjoy the little things around you , and majestic things above and below you . On a clear night sky a billion stars twinkle and you realize the concept of just how tiny we are , the occasional flying fish gliding over and through the waves sometimes for a distance of fifty feet . The ships bow wake at night , cutting through phosphor that lies on the surface of the water and creating a light show equalling Aurora borealis . Sighting a shark , or a group of Orka's. The morning air so fresh . Dolphins playing around the bow of the ship . "They do that to clean their skin "Reg offered , Alan chipped in , "In the days of sail it was a sign of good fortune to have dolphins on the bow " , then the most ludicrous offer "Now I don't know if it's TRUE" Pete went on , "but , in fog they used to guide the ship ". We all doubled over with laughter , "Well that's what they used to say ". Pete defended his statement . "Give it a rest Pete ". Days later , Land HO

Chapter 8

I was in the galley as usual but dropped everything and scurrying to the deck thought, shit, why cant I be the first to spot land and looked out on this magnificent spectacle. Where?. Well, the spotter answered sheepishly, I thought I, " There ! There I" It was confirmed, . "Africa ". the boson approaching confirming ."We are putting in at Libreville ". As we got closer we noticed two native fishermen in an open type sailing dinghy with a black sail . "They use black sails so they don't frighten the fish" offered Pete the Oracle . As we got closer it wasn't a sail , it was a Manta ray they had caught and had rigged to the mast , "Pete !. Tha knows nowt ". He took the jibes well . Closer in to shore it looked exactly like it does on the movies . We were all brought back to the present with , "Get back to it lads " from the boson . Later that afternoon we anchored in Libreville sound , half a mile off shore . "How are we ", somebody started to say but was interrupted by the boson ," Get to the lifeboat station lads . Captains putting on a liberty boat for you . We'll use the starboard 2 , give us a bit of practice just in case we ever have to abandon ship" . We had just got up to the boat deck when the second mate intervened . "Hold everything lads , we need the gangway setting up and lowering . The agent is paying the captain a visit" . No sooner had we got it rigged , across the bay came the launch , four on board ,One of them was blonde , long hair , blonde ! . "Hey , look at this lads ! ," We know we know , we've seen her" . It only turns out the agent had brought out his teenage daughter . Is he mad . "Oh effin heck lads , she's wearing shorts ". The boson was screaming his nuts off , "Get yourselves back up here and launch this lifeboat" but who cared . There was everything we wanted right here , A Girl ! And she's blonde !. "Look "shouted the boson "It doesn't take all of you . I want you all back up here and one of you to go and secure the launch ". After you Reg . No after you Pete . Eight men scrambling and pushing and wrestling for the gangway and not one for the lifeboat cheered the boson up no end . "I said one of you ", but he was talking to himself . The wrestling ensued , It ended I was told when I climbed over the bulwark and jumped onto the gangway . No mean feat . Making my way down to meet the princess with the ash blonde hair . She comes , she , sheesh . What a pair of tits , legs up to her ! What was up there ? I had only got to the tits section on the girls I had dated . Cant for the life of me understand why they never dated me again . The boat came alongside the gangway ,and ,being given a line . I made it fast . Helped one onto the swinging gantry step , then another , here comes the treat , "I will help my daughter thank you seaman" . Oh no your not thought I , and for good measure I shook the gantry step to make it unstable enough for him to grab the rail of the gangway . "Better you leave it to me sir , we don't want any accidents " . Now, my princess of Africa I mused . She looked nervous having to negotiate from the bobbing launch to the tiny square which formed the bottom of the gangway . But offering my arms for stability she half stepped half fell into my arms . Thank you lord thank you . Its times like these that make up for all the things that go wrong . The softness of her breasts upon my chest , although fleeting , was the highlight of my being . She released herself from me with a smile as her father steadied her and she turned to climb the gangway steps . I had offered my hand to the remaining chap on the launch but seeing that bottom in those shorts wiggling up the steps I completely forgot and as he reached for my steadying hand , it wasn't , if you know what I mean . Splosh ! , I quickly turned to see him with one foot on the gantry and the other in the water . Looking daggers at me . "Steady now Sir we don't want you falling in" didn't seem to help matters as he said something in French , for my ears only which didn't sound nice, but extremely emphatic. I enjoyed watching him struggle up the gangway and looking to the boatman. A black man with the broadest smile, wink and snigger, I returned his approval with a chuckle and shrug of the shoulders, The sound carried up the gangway causing wet foot to try turning to see who was laughing but I wobbled the gangway and he quickly turned to secure his grip. I was still in raptures when I climbed back to deck, not realizing at first the faces that were glaring at me. When they picked me up and held me over the side threatening to drop me into the briny for my misdeeds I was half laughing as I pleaded for life to go on. The cheery banter was broken by the boson, "Look, are we going to launch this lifeboat or

don't you want to go ashore tonight ".
Say no more , shore leave , I'm your man .
What happened next as men welded together in one cause , deployed the lifeboat with such dexterity the boson being half a yard behind in his guiding orders gave up and .let us get on with it .
We were a team . One goal , Out she swung , a little off on the winches but hey !. We had sent Pete and big nasty bugger down with the boat . To start the engine , disconnect the blocks and bring it round to the gangway . Yes , to start the er ! To start , "It wont start".Pete shouted up .
Have you done this have you done that . The information being shared was mind blowing in that few moments of , Brumm ! , she runs and a hooray erupted from our lungs that must have caused everyone in Libreville to stop and look

where the sound had come from . Probably the fastest , definitely the fastest I had ever cleared off the evening meal pots . Lead me to the promised land , ablutions in progress only two pieces of toilet paper required , getting to be a doddle this shaving lark . Clean shirt and Jean's and I was on deck . The boson walked toward us as we milled around the amidships gangway . The look on his face wasn't encouraging nor was his opening comment . "Sorry John , you can't go ashore , the mate says you haven't got enough experience yet " . " No , and it doesn't look as though I'll fucking get any either " . He went on ," He's only looking after your interests , he was even doubtful about the rest of you after Los Palmas" . At last , seeing the ones drop their gaze to the floor gave me a fairly good idea who had caused such a mess . "Rest of you line up at the mates door for your advance against your wages ". I remained on deck to watch them , having received their advance , to bid them farewell , don't get too drunk . I got a few sorry you can't , its for the best , maybe next time , your not missing anything was the most insulting . Of course I am , I'm missing everything . Thought , not spoken . I waved to the motley crew as the lifeboat , carrying the blessed , pulled away heading for Shangri la . Trooping back to the aft . "Where are you going" . I turned to face the voice but my angry face soon disappeared as it was the second mate . "I was just "." It's not a holiday you know . The ship needs a watch on deck at all times ". Yes sir , then No sir as the drubbing continued .

Eventually, whether he had run out of steam or was panicking to return to his whisky bottle, his sanctuary giving me reprieve. Bill had stayed behind, he hadn't felt well enough to go ashore "Cheer up lad, go and get a jumper on, it might get cold later on I'll cover the watch ". Cold ,, in this heat. Experience, why don't I learn. My progress was checked on every hour and when the boson(showed I inquired," how long ?". " Until they come back ?" his answer anticipated my question . Well, this is a right ta ta , I chastised to myself but was disturbed from my grumbles by , "Good evening son". Who's this, I had been on the boat a month but never seen him before, "nice night he went on ". Er yes, is it, oops I mean it is Sir yes. I've not seen you around". "Yes I know, I'm the captain ". I didn't know whether to bow, salute or what . " Any trouble with the watch " he went on ," Er no Sir everything's fine ". " Good " then " Well done for volunteering to stay behind" . I'll fucking kill them I thought , everything I have done and they still insist on treating me like a leper when it comes to trust . "Yes sir that's alright , I didn't want to go ashore anyway , just got caught up in the situation" . Lying bugger John . "Oh well , good evening" and off he went . So , yer buggers . Yer didn't want to nursemaid a minor . The boson in on it too . Can't believe it , just can't . I'm going to rub shit on my face so when they come back wanting to hug they'll get more than they bargained for . Yes I'll show em . One thirty , no sign , two thirty still no sign . Where can they be . At last , a torchlight on the water , good distance away but yep its ours , zero three forty five hours where have they been ? . As the lifeboat swung in at the bottom of the gangway , its instinctive , something's wrong . No singing , counting them on board I enquired . "What's wrong with you lot . Where's Pete" ? . "We've been looking for him , that's why we're late coming back" . Just when you could do without it . Up pops the second mate . "Anyone drunk Parks" , I reminded him , Parkin sir , "Well carry on"." Just a minute sir , the liberty boats back but there is one missing ", on inquiry ," Pete sir , apparently the crew have been searching for him but to no avail ". The eyes , I could feel them burning into my back . I later reasoned to them that if he was in trouble it's better for someone in authority to know . And besides . How is he supposed to get back if you've got the lifeboat . The light came on in there eyes as the penny dropped .. Thank goodness , no cuddling this time as they retired aft . What a difference to Los Palmas . The boson came up from aft . " John , I need to ask you a favour" . "Is it to volunteer to stay on board so people don't have to babysit me" . "Who told ? " ." Yer doing well but don't spoil it . I need you to cover till six am then you can have twenty four hours just pleasing yourself , how's that sound " . "Great ! . Sorry for what I said , yes I'll do it "." Good lad " . It got to four in the morning and I was on a different planet . Sleep had cuckolded me twice and even waving my arms , doing a funny dance , stretching my face , were all failing rapidly . I need sleep . Reprieve came in the form of good old Reg , My mate . This hallowed breed set in a silver sea . "John , Go and get yer head down before you fall down ".I thanked him but inquired ." What do you think happened to Pete? ". "No idea , we were all drinking having a laugh . He was fancying a native girl who he had a dance with and the next thing we knew they had disappeared . So the only thing I can think of is he's got her for the night". Not quite . Turned out , as we found out later . Pete left the bar with her , thinking she was taking him to her place for a quickie . She led him off the main street straight into the arms of four youths who beat him unconscious . Robbed him of his wallet , and then stripped him naked and took his clothes . A few hours later , at daybreak . A group of nuns from the missionary, found him lying on the ground. They managed to revive him and then took him to their mission, cleaned his wounds and provided him with a makeshift pair of trousers and a T shirt to hide his modesty. They handed him to the Police who then brought him back to the ship. The two policemen then tried to usurp money from the Captain for bringing him back on some charge or other. The Captain had seen all this malarkey before and threatened to contact their superior. They couldn't get off the ship fast enough. Ten thirty I was awakened." Captain wants to see everyone on deck". It was then I was informed by the crew as to what had transpired with Pete. "Is he ok"." Well he's a bit shook up and badly bruised". We arrived on deck facing the amidships galley . The Captain , first second and third mate all in attendance trooped out ." Were in for it "whispered Reg . He never swore once but even the officers who stood alongside him looked gravely concerned , even though the drubbing was aimed at the rest of us . It ended with . "Get the liberty boat shipped , you will not be needing it again ". Reminded us that we were all to have a weeks pay docked and went back to his cabin . "Hey boson does that mean me as well , I was on board "." Best leave it son until he calms down . He's got to enter this kerfuffle into the ships log and that's a blight on him as well as everyone else" . "Does that mean I can't have the twenty four hours then "? "I'll see what I can do but , no , it wont be twenty four hours and hey yer cheeky bugger! You went off duty early ". I laughed and dodged as he took a playful swing at me with his boot . "So how long can I have ". Be up before tea . Six and a half hours . After returning to my bunk and tossing and turning I let my mind slip back to Sharpness .

Chapter 9

It was the day we had been dreading . We had been instructed on how and how not , to launch a lifeboat , and to us , both seemed pretty similar . Our tutor for the event was Morrison who insisted on parading his gold braid , white hat , and collar and tie and strangely the Merchant naval tie . " Right you lot listen up . Now we've discussed this in the class till it should be second nature . Now don't forget I am going to take each step slowly and he emphasised slowly . Do you understand ". Just as slowly we all chirped . "We understand " . He looked at us realizing we were mimicking , "Look lads this is " and went on for ten minutes until we were sick of it ,"so let's pay attention "." Because the lifeboat is longer than the davits we have to do a swinging motion . We pull back into the ship , the stern of the lifeboat , and then swing the other davit so the bow is now clear and free on the outside of that davit . We then swing the stern of the lifeboat forward , past its davit and then swing back so the boat is now free to launch ". He was bemused that we had done it perfectly . "Right now comes the hard bit . You must keep the boat level whilst winching it down" , again almost perfect , even we were completely amazed at how well things were going ."

Right . Now when I blow this whistle I am going to shout abandon ship" . Blew he did , but not one man moved ." Lads your supposed to be abandoning ship and jump for the rat lines ". And that was the crux of our plight . With the davits at full stretch the rat lines were some six feet away from the ships side and a thirty foot drop to the lifeboat . " Right once more " and he blew and yes , we didn't move . "Oh this is ridiculous . Your supposed to be men , your acting like a bunch of girlies ". "Right the first one to jump can go to the social club tonight ". Two lads , both jumping together but for one ratline . One grabbed the line forcing the second one to grab the first lad by the legs . Well , trying to sort themselves out and seeing a pair of trousers heading south we just were beside ourselves with laughter . "Get a hold of the effin rope yer daft bugger" . At last the message got through to the one on the pants and he swooped his grip to the rope and slid at break neck speed down the rat line and screamed with pain when at the bottom . "You alright lad "? . "I've burnt my hands Sir" . "Yes lads , don't slide down the rope go down hand over hand or under as the case may be ". We watched the duo but were still reluctant especially having witnessed the guy with the rope burns and he was definitely in a lot of pain ." Right you lot had better get this exercise done or I'm keeping you here for another six weeks training so first three line up . Jump . second three line up . Jump ". Until all of us were in the lifeboat ." Right lads climb onto shore and I will be down in a minute

".." Arh ! It's alright for him to use the stairs" said one lad but had to eat his words when Morrison came almost abseiling down the rat line . "There lads that's how you do it ". One or two passed comment pretty fit guy . We wasted no time in getting ready for the social . There was just one snag . So that the locals could identify us we could not wear casuals , we had to go in uniform . We shuffled into the village hall . There were about four girls probably a bit older than us but you never can tell . Accompanied by four guys , couple of husbands five or six women of varying age . And of course twenty of us lot . The matriarch of the evening came over to greet ." Boy's how lovely to see you . I'm sorry we haven't got partners for you all but if you would care to follow me you can help yourselves to a biscuit or two and possibly a cup of tea" . Who's fucking big idea was it to come here . She's a right Ponsonby forthright Snodgrass . Oh it'll be fine once the music starts ." Ladies and gentlemen ". The matriarch was now on stage caressing the only thing that wouldn't be repelled by her touch . The microphone . "Pray take your partners for a quick step ". Are they for real . To prove it about four couples took to the floor . We could see this was going to be a breath-taking experience but the biscuits were proving popular with us and as we had walked three miles to get here we may as well pocket a few for the walk home . One of the lads approached one of the girls for a dance and was quickly surrounded by the female elders who spirited the girl from reach . So that's it . Were here as trophies of generosity for the Sunday service and who should walk through the door to confirm it , The vicar . He came over , welcoming our arrival . "Perhaps you could join us at the Sunday congregation" ." Sorry sir but we have exams" ." Surely not on Sunday ". No sir , He's done his homework this one ," We have to study on Sunday before the Monday exam ". He stepped back as if the devil himself had come calling resisting the temptation of raising his crucifix to safeguard himself from us . "Well other boys have done it" . Think , think ." Yes Sir but the curriculum is now linked to two exams on the Monday whereas in the past it was on different days". Deflated , defeated and reeling from confusion then the hammer blow . "In fact sir , quite a few of the lads are a bit panicky that they wont have

time to study so. Unfortunately , we wont be able to stay as long as we would have liked ". Turning he muttered enjoy the rest of the evening and seeked sanctuary in the folds of the congregation ." Right lads are we ready " , and to a man a resounding . "Aye" . "Thank your for inviting us , it's been lovely , thank you for the tea" . We made for the door to the return comment . Singularly ," Pease come again ". Not on your sweet Nellie or words to that effect . Tracking back to camp we realised we had scoffed and pocketed all the biscuits. Peals of laughter brought an extrusion of airborne crumbs from us making us double up in hysterics .
"It's not what you've told the vicar . It's the way you ruined their evening . There were no biscuits left!". At this . Our

receiving a bollocking line up gave way to laughter . So emphatically that the officer cracked into laughter with us ." Now look" , he managed to steady himself , "we cant have biscuits ruining our reputation " and then broke down into uncontrollable laughter and we joined with him wholeheartedly . Tears now streaming from his face along with the rest of us ." Get yourselves out of my sight and consider yourselves" , he couldn't finish it and we filed out of his office. His peels of laughter challenging ours . No more was ever said of the event under a strict warning of silence .

Chapter 10

The sound of the anchor being weighed brought me wide awake from my reminiscing. Looking at my watch, Three

PM . Still got an hour and a half I thought but my inquisitiveness got the better of me and I went up on deck . "Oh , just the man "greeted the bosun ." Nip down and put a brew on for the lads" ." What's happening bosun " . He volunteered ,"Were moving down the coast to where we pick up a crew of natives . Then on to pick up our cargo , look sharp there's a good lad" . Tea over but questions abound . "Don't like the sound of Natives occupying the ship" . "Yeh and where are they going to do there shitting " . "Awe Pete for fuck sake shut it" . Tha's caused enough trouble for one day " . Which silenced Pete but his accuser went on ," tha's lost us all a weeks pay so just shut it " . Silence , then , "Where are they going to eat and sleep . Well I'm not sharing my bunk with anybody unless she's got big tits". The laughter that ensued released the tension. In walks the boson " John go into the focsle head and get Reg to give you a hand setting the scrambling nets". I went through the motions of pretending to know what he was on about but hadn't got a clue until Reg explained. During the war they used to throw scrambling nets over the side to allow the maximum number of men to clamber aboard so they could get underway before they were picked off by U boats and the like. We unshipped the nets. Gosh, they weigh a ton. "Wait while we have to get them over the side" said Reg. Two hours down the coast we stopped and waited for the crew. There was no movement whatsoever and the beach village seemed abandoned. Is this the right place someone offered. The villages along this stretch of coast compete for the contracts to load the ships . Suddenly , Ants , no men , swarmed off the beach and into canoes heading for us . "Hey up lads lets get the nets over the side ". I wish I had had a net instead of a Jacob's ladder when I had to board her . Far safer I mused . Then they were upon us . Scrambling up the nets and over the side . They made their way down into the open cargo holds and set to , arranging their accommodation for the next two or three weeks . Once the natives were on board , we retrieved the nets and the ship moved on to our rendezvous where we were to take on the logs . "Ten thousand tons of logs is a lot of trees" I offered ". Yes and multiply that with the amount of ships loading and it's a disaster for the jungle life" . How poignant that observation was . Especially its deliverer . Big nasty bugger . Neil . "Do we have to feed this lot boson ", Alan asked . "No , they look after themselves . If they were to eat our food they would be sick just the same as if we tried to eat theirs" . An hour later we stopped and weighed anchor . Here we were at last . The boson called us together . "Right I've got some good news and some very good news . We don't have to load the logs the natives do it all so . Stop your cheering . So , we are going to take this opportunity to make us proud of our ship . Tomorrow morning were going to paint her from stem to stern . Superstructure, the lot . What no questions "? The boson went on . "We've got six chipping hammers so first thing tomorrow , the men with the most experience of using a chipping hammer . I want you to start from the bridge down to the deck ". Hmmm everyone seemed a bit bemused but no complaints . Well certainly about the heat . That's going to be bloody hot wearing the masks . More solemnity . The boson Rose to the challenge ," So far you haven't struck a bat and you've been at sea, what , a month "! He moved up a gear and I wasn't the only one that recognised the arrival and delivery that was sprinkled gratuitously with eloquent four letter words which went on and on until finally . "Alright ! " ." Aye boson " rapped smartly from our lips .

" Ever used a chipping hammer John" Reg inquired and went on . " Here let me show you . Put this mask on , don't want any shale going into your eyes " . Once knew a man", but didn't hear the rest as we were joined by the third mate . "What are you two up to ". "I was just going to ". "Oh no your not " he went on , " You can take those glasses off lad , and you Reg you ought to know better , he'll have the ship looking like a colander if you put one of those in his hands" . "But he's got to learn" Reg protested weakly . "Well let him practice putting holes in somebody else's ship . Here , I've got a job for you" . I murmured under my breath as he retreated into the wheelhouse ," Go down and make me a drink of tea" . He reappeared with mug in hand and uttered exactly what I had predicted . To the tune of it's a long way to tipperary played on the Jack hammers , its surprising how you can put a tune to noise and it's a long way to tipperary seems to fit most , I shuffled discontentedly back to our galley kitchen . On arrival back at the wheelhouse the third mate thanked me , his attitude softened and asked . "Have you been in the wheelhouse before . Only to deliver cups of tea" , damm , I could have bit my lip . "Well ", he went on stifling a smile at my comment . "Go and stand at the helm . Feel the weight of the wheel , I passed it from side to side but negligible movement . You have to control the ship and maintain a course if possible within ten degrees that's obviously subject to the weather " . "If the sea is heavy we have to allow the bow to swing as she takes a wave and then bring her back the other way as we ride the lee" . This is the life , this is what an enquiring mind needed , So , he went on . "If you were at the wheel and had to release , say , to port , twenty degrees , to bring her back on course how many degrees would you adjust to starboard ". I was even astounded by getting the answer correct ." Tell you what lad , when we are loaded , remind me and you can join me and the helmsman on the bridge . When your off normal duties of course ". A resounding , "Yes Sir ! That would be fantastic" ." Why don't you go and have a look at what the natives are up to" , "Thank you Sir " and left the wheelhouse as if I owned it . "Stop , ." Not that way , they're chipping out there , use the rear companionway" . I looked but didn't see . he strode across to a door at the rear of the wheelhouse ,opened it , and ushered me out . . I wonder if he meant it , have I buggered up my chance of the offer he made Oh John you are a stupid irresponsible , little realizing I was exercising my thoughts aload ." Hullo, that's a sad look for a young man to carry even more so when he has to give it an excuse aloud" . It was the Captain . Don't salute , don't bow . Oh heck ! Can this day get any worse and offered a feeble ," Sorry sir" . "What's wrong won't they let you loose on the chipping . Steer clear of it lad as long as you can , it's a devil of a job and likely as not the boson will be chasing you to sweep up the fash " (metal flakes of rust) . But , he went on ," I see no reason why you shouldn't have a go at painting , ever used a bosons chair before "? . " We had a practice session with one at Sharpness ". "Old Vindie , now there's a ship for you . Manned by men ,Men were half starved in those days and poorly paid ". " Nothing , if the cargo was damaged" , "but they could handle that canvas like a bullfighter handles his Cape , even in the roughest sea "." How long have you been at sea Sir." "Long enough to know I have been talking too long" and with a quick , "cheer up lad ". He turned and went back to his cabin . Should have asked him if I was being docked a weeks pay . Oh come on John , put some life into it . Another brainwave . I had noticed a second tea urn that someone had stored in the focsle head when we were getting the scrambling nets out . Going forward, I retrieved the urn , took it to our galley and gave it a really good clean . Filled it with fresh water , beckoned two of the natives , who we had decided , we shall call them Johnnie .

Slightly confusing when there are forty of them, who were on deck and I got them to carry the urn forward. Stopped off at the chief stewards cabin. Oh dear, sozzled again, He was never sober. Never ate, just drank beer all the time the assistant steward Jeff informed me when we had been chatting on deck one night. "Hi chief, have you got any ice we could have" .and explained the reason for the request. " See Jeff, tell him I said to give you some from the freezer ". Armed now with ice in the urn the two urn carriers had become four. Right johnnie's follow me. I set up the urn amidships and informed the chippers by hand signal I had got them a drink. The cooled waters of paradise ,"Cor ! I could just dive into this head first " said the first to taste. Similar comments from the others who followed by example . Boson appeared, that boson can smell anything , downed a dram of water and said , "By , that's good . Who's idea was this then "?."John's " came a couple of replies . He refilled his cup . "We will have these every day" ,and slurped his way through the second helping . On the third he warned us , "Now don't drink too much of this all in one go or you'll upset your stomach" . Everyone laughed at the obvious . Oh boson . Tha's a rum un . "Right lads back to work ". The following morning , the Johnnie's were chatting excitedly and gestured to us . Coming across the bay were two motor boats and dragging behind them a tier of logs . My word , look at them , they cant wait to get started on the loading . The boats came , with their logs , alongside and made fast the ropes . Within minutes the natives had manned the davits and were preparing to bring aboard the first log . It may have been the controls for the winches sticking , but the first tree to come aboard wasn't going down into the hold without a fight . The tree caught the pantry doors . Smashing them like matchwood . The boys operating the davit winches quickly got the tree under control and although struggling with the length and weight of this colossal tree trunk finally managed to coax it down , what appeared to be a cat flap opening , in relation to the size of the tree . With that we returned to our duties and sure enough I was put on cleaning up the fash chippings , "where do we" , "Over the side lad "the bosun intercepting my question . Oh well , this is going to be easier than I thought . Then had a brain wave . The natives just sat around at night twiddling their thumbs . So I gathered up the fash into piles alongside the handrails amidships . Most of the Africans were camping below but some were also on deck . That night I gestured for the ones below deck to be called on deck and then having grabbed a handful of the fash slung it overboard . The resulting splash landing on the phosphor set off a hundred flashing lights much to the delight of the natives whereupon they jostled to gather a handful of the fash and repeat the light show . Fascinating how little things …. . The head man of the village seeing Charlie the chief steward in his braid , had set up camp outside Charlie's porthole much to the amusement of the other officers . Whilst

I was cleaning around amidships, Jeff, the assistant steward called from the starboard side of the ship. I walked over to join him, and leaned over the side of the ship. "John, don't, and I mean don't turn around just yet but this guy behind us is the head man. "He's having a wash in sea water on deck. When you turn to go back over to port have a look at his tool". and his gestured glance to his groin had nothing to do with a Maccano set. I nodded, "See you Jeff", turned and. "What the ", I wish I hadn't looked, He had got more to play with than I had to walk with ! ". Effin hell, fu '! Jeez !". I had a sudden urge to ask what's the food they eat. As I crossed over to port the third mate looking at the expression on my face said, "bet you've seen it then ". with a broad grin on his face ." Seen it , I nearly tripped over it ". Causing us both to laugh . Then , more thoughtful he said , "I used to travel these waters a lot and on the quayside you could see the mothers pulling their baby's tail. Because they believed that if their child has a big nob he will grow up to be a big chief ". "Seriously" I inquired , he nodded with an emphatic "Yes ! ". Well mum , yer might have constantly mopped my tears but I wish you'd have spent a little less time up their and a bit more time down below . During tea that night I said . "Hey ! Did you see ". And as if to a man "We've all seen it ". Came the reply . Fucking hell I thought , Has Jeff been selling tickets . None of us had any money so that thought went straight out of the window or should I now say porthole . When we needed tobacco or fags we simply lined up outside the chief stewards cabin he then got what you requested . Beer maximum four bottles , empties came back before you could have four more , obviously this was once a week . Tobacco , a tin at a time . Fags , two hundred for ten Bob or 50 p in todays money . I particularly was enjoying smoking Pall Mall . The American brand . Only drawback , if you put them any where but your shirt pocket they had a tendency to get crushed . And , the drawback with having them in your shirt pocket was , people helping themselves to your fags . Can be quite annoying going through a packet and you've had five or six out of the twenty . I'm going to buy a shirt with button down pockets I promised myself . First port of call . The ship was starting to fill with its cargo of timber and as promised I finally got my hands on a paint brush and was given the task of painting the lower accommodation outside structure . "Bloody hell boson ", one of the crew piped ," Couldnt you have got a better colour than baby shit beige" . "It'll look nice once its dry" came his reply . But it didn't . "John , what you doing , you've got more paint on you than what you've got on the bulkhead . Its not the Mona Lisa your painting" . Not being acquainted with the lady I asked whose she ? ." Don't you start" . "No boson , honestly , who's she? ". " It's a famous painting in Paris" , he replied . "Go and get yourself cleaned up . Afterthought , "Oh ! And knock us up some of that ice water" . I daren't tell him that the lads for a laugh , as they were passing me , had pushed their paint brush into my ear , up my nose , and painted my hands . He would have clapped us all in irons and stopped another weeks pay .

Chapter 11

Daily , fresh tiers of logs were brought out to the ship and there seemed rapid progress with the loading . The natives worked tirelessly throughout the heat of the day from eight AM finishing each day with the last log coming aboard around six PM. The lads who were riding the logs on the water slinging , were fine whilst there were plenty of logs to stand on . The problem came when there was only a few . The problem being Sharks . They would charge the log that the guy was standing on and cause a backwash from the side of the ship thus spinning the log

. On a couple of occasions the inevitable happened and they had guys on deck with a rope around the guy below ready to haul him out of the water . Makes you shudder to watch . So close . The painting was coming along a treat . Sadly the colour was abysmal "Who picked this bloody colour " being aired on numerous occasions . Too numerous for the boson and he defended his pride and joy by answering , "Would you rather have rust" . My day on the bosons chair , painting over the side was hilarious . We rigged a pole onto the brush so that we were able to paint down to the plimsoll line without becoming bait for you know who . Getting the brush into the paint pot and the chair spinning you couldnt do anything but just laugh . This dilemma after the second day was solved when the boson, who by this time was sick and tired of our shenanigans, had a quick chat with the boatmen who were bringing out the logs. Once they had tied the logs off a couple of the lads would climb into the boats with their pot of paint and paint brushes and painted the remainder with ease, hey presto ! Problem, What problem !. The cargo holds were filling rapidly and came the day we would be parting with our colonial brethren. We sealed the holds but to our surprise more logs were being brought out. We were to fill all deck space. The order came from the first mate and for access we had to rig a gantry step and walkway across the logs. With having so many extra people on board our water supply was rapidly disappearing and our captain did a deal with the captain of a

German ship to take on fresh water from them . Now , The German ships radio operators were female . Our captain invited a number of the German officers over for lunch . Halfway through the meal the visiting radio officer excused herself , having to return to her ship . The exit from the saloon took her past the chief stewards cabin . Charlie being in a drunken state thought all his prayers had been answered and tried to drag the girl into his cabin . She was strong enough to resist his challenge and broke free . Coming out on deck where we were rigging for taking on board the water from the German ship . She shouted something to her crewmates . . The mood quickly changed amongst the German crew . We were oblivious of the event so suspected nothing . Jeff the assistant steward had observed the incident between her and Charlie . We duly took on the water and the German ship pulled away . We first noticed the difference in the water that evening when Reg said ," bloody hell John , what have you put in this tea , it tastes lousy ". This was supported by the boson who came into the mess and said "don't drink the water lads . The buggers have given us salt water and it's also contaminated the fresh water we had left ". Dilemma , what do we drink for the next five days till we can put into Dakar and flush the tanks ? Charlie knew ! We were informed by Jeff , He had eight cases of beer brought to his cabin for his own consumption and eight cases in the bond room should he run out . "He cant leave this ship , he owes them too much" Neil remarked which brought a resounding Aye ! ." That's the last one "! . The third officer declared the loading completed The ship was overflowing with logs piled four times higher than the guard rails some fifteen feet above deck level . We looked like a floating log cabin . "Weigh anchor lads ".the boson continued "We are dropping off the African lot and then pushing on for Dakar ". I was in the mess room . Where else . The following day at sea we were in a steep swell when all of a sudden the ship heeled over violently catching everyone by surprise . Running up on deck I had visions of us turning turtle and having to abandon ship . Everyone else had the same suspicions as crew , firemen from the engine room , engineers the lot , all to a man were on deck with the same intent . All except good old Charlie, he had stayed behind to go down with his beer. Then a related message came from the bridge. "It's all right it's all right, The cargo's moved. Everything is fine". Fine or not, with the ship at an angle of forty five degrees not many slept well that night, nor for the next few nights. Dakar, at last. Fresh water, The beer taste in the tropical heat, our substitute for water for the Last four and a half days, was rank. A bitter memory if you'll forgive the pun which, honestly, wasn't intended. But fresh water to drink. The boson cheerily shouted, "John", I finished it," Go and make a mug of tea ", the cheer from everyone proved unanimous and for devilment I shouted, "Or would you rather have a beer". Later midday I was called over to the side of the ship by Reg

." Look" nodding in the general direction of the dock ."don't laugh what ever you do " ,All the hustle and bustle of dock life had come to a standstill . Each individual , and there were many , caught up in prayer . "They're praying to their God" Reg went on , "they have to face Mecca . Those what they are kneeling on are prayer mats ". The ritual was carried out to a man . "What's Mecca" . "The holy city of Muhammad . I think that's right" ! . he concluded . "We'll be leaving soon , we're just waiting for a few stores Charlie's ordered" . "Beer ". everyone shouted . Yes it was beer but also the most wonderful fresh bread I have ever tasted before or since . The tugs came alongside, took our hawsers and nudged us into the channel for departure . "Hey lads ", Pete , who else . "I've just been on the bridge and overheard second and third (officers) saying were pulling into Casa Blanca" ." Oh that'll be interesting for you John ", Alan said . "One side of the street is French , the other side of the street is Moroccan . Two entirely different cultures , make sure if you do go ashore you stick to the Moroccan side . It costs a bomb , even for a water on the French side" . From dropping off our African crew I had been handed a magazine by one of the engineers . I quickly hid it from view until I was in the sanctuary of my cabin whereupon glancing through it , I was disappointed there were no pin up girls pictures . Just one or two articles . One of them was about Clint Walker alias Cheyenne Bodie who apparently was a merchant seaman before becoming an actor . Having read the article , Alan's comments of Casa Blanca , apparently were not shared as enthusiastically by Clint who , when realizing his wallet was being lifted . Threw the perpetrator to the ground and was attacked by several of the street traders for defending his money and escaped , luckily ,with cuts and bruises . So , It was with mixed feelings I pondered the dilemma of going ashore . "Ah ! . You'll be fine" when I aired my views to the crew one evening . You'll be with us ! Jovially I chided , "Well I'm definitely not going then ". Bringing a hearty laugh to the conversation .

Chapter 12

We pulled into Casa Blanca . No sooner had we deployed our lines and the gangway . The seven tribes of Sinbad were upon us . Opening their blankets and marketing their wares in the very limited space we had left on deck . The boson called me over and said . "Get a couple of the lads and get them to clear this lot off the ship" . I thought oh I'll do that . "Come along chaps , Come on , gather up your things" , no movement whatsoever . Are they deaf , so , tried speaking a little louder and made the mistake of putting my hand on the shoulder of one of them . The next thing I knew he had a knife to my face and I dare not move , then ,suddenly nor did he . We both noticed at the same time . A baling hook was in front of his eye . The knife clattered on the deck and he froze . I only noticed at that point that on the other end of the baling hook was none other than big nasty bugger . Neil . With a one hand sweeping motion , he dispatched our unwelcome visitors, who hurriedly gathered their stuff and scurried, like rats from a sinking ship. Save for the one who had brandished the knife. Neil had hold of the guys gallabia and carried him, protesting, to the gangway. The guy, once released, ran halfway down the gangway, turned and then gave Neil a mouthful of abuse. Neil turned to me, "Gather his things into the blanket and bring them here". I complied, He held them up for the man on the gangway to see and the ones at the bottom of the gangway waiting for him, to get his goods. As the man came forward to collect them, Neil released his grip. The blanket along with its contents splashed into the water. The screaming that ensued, both from shore and gangway reminded me of slaughter day on the farm . "Right John , that's how you get rid of them" . I was still a bit shaken but , surprisingly, not for myself . Neil went on ," it's the only language they understand . Now , how's about a mug of tea son" . The big nasty bugger was no more . .Later that afternoon , the guy who had lost his wares was back , This time accompanied by two policemen . The third mate greeted them but they were being very threatening in their actions ,demanding recompense . Just when it looked like the police were getting the upper hand who should walk down on deck but the Captain . The third mate started to make an attempt to introduce the Captain to the police . But the Captain totally ignored the police asking ." What are these people doing on my ship" ." Apparently " , the third mate started . "No ! . What are these people doing on my ship" . The captain turned to the policemen and the trader , crooked his finger in a follow me gesture . He walked them to the gangway stood aside , bowed slightly and with a wave of his hand ushered them onto the gangway . They turned to protest but the Captain hooked the no entry chain across the gangway walked up to the third mate and invited him to join him in his cabin . No shouting no arguing no threatening he had dispatched all three without uttering a word . This might be a shit tip ship . But some of the people on it are second to none . I felt a sense of belonging and was proud . It's not what it appears , its who you are and how you deal with it . Oh ! Little sweet old lady from careers . You've done it again ."

Right this time we don't want any trouble whatsoever", the first mate had called to his cabin all who were going ashore." Any one of you, I don't care who it is. You'll have your kit and caboodle dumped on the dock and you can make your own way home. Do I make my self clear ". Nearly to a man. "Yes Sir, one O "." Right line up for your advance on your wages and sign the book". At last ashore in a foreign country, we trooped down the gangway but on the dock I experienced my legs were not working correctly and the rest of the crew laughed, we've all done that. Because I hadn't been on terra firma my body was anticipating movement, the sensation quickly disappeared however, along with the accompanying nausea. The street, once we cleared the dock gates was exactly as had been described . The French to the left sat in their street coffee shops , white suits abound and the colours and elegance of the dresses their ladies wore was like nothing I had ever seen , even on films . To the right , the Souk . It ran all the way up the street . Carpets , jewellery . Clothing bags ,spices it was like a gigantic open air department store with two , sometimes three Arabs per stall although they weren't really stalls either . Their chatter became deafening as they vied for our business everything looked vibrant but I noticed , it soon lost its appeal once ignored .Strange . Shirts were being thrust into our arms , hats , trousers ,. "Shirts , button down pockets" I inquired . I was half dragged by the shirt seller to his stall . "All right all right "but my protests were just as effective as they had been on the ship . He could smell a sale and I was his lunch ." Button down pockets , No , not those . Button , button no not stripes" . Pete said , "Here let me try , I speak the lingo ". Salvation at last . "You havey shirty with buttony ". I just burst out laughing . "Pete ! Yer full of crap "! Then to my astonishment the bloke on the stall ran behind and dragged five or six shirts off a shelf , every one had button down pockets . Pete picked up each shirt in turn ," how muchey ". Every time the guy gave a price , nah and waved his hand sideways to emphasis his disinterest . " Right John let's walk away" . The guy was round to block our escape in a flash and the price now was half the first quote . Same ritual from Pete again . After the third time of walking away I ended up with three shirts for the price of one . Inevitably , in that heat . You just have to take the shade which came in the shape of a cafe serving beer . I wasn't a drinker , well , not like this lot so I soon started falling behind as their drinks disappeared . Mine , on the other hand started to stack up . "C'mon John , get em down you . Let's move on lads ", . I was glad when we were back out in the sun again , but felt a bit woozy ." Let's get some thing to eat" . Reg said , are you alright lad , I nodded , "you'll feel better with some grub inside you" . What a meal for just a few pennies , the courses just kept coming , Alan was in his element ordering all food known to man and the waiters each time he ordered poured him more wine . How is he holding it all down , I was amazed but he just kept going . With the food inside me I was feeling a lot better, "Hey lads ", Reg had been chatting with the barman ," He's just been telling me there is a night club just round the corner said we ought to try it . Finish up were going ". Outside it was dusk . Crickey , how long had we been eating . "C'mon its round here . Ah! there it is look . It's down these steps".. We walked into a large room with booths around the walls on three sides . On the other wall there was a stage upon which a band playing fifties music . In the centre of the room probably fifteen tables . And , tucked in the corner , yes , a bar . We started to make a beeline for it but was intercepted by a smartly dressed waiter . "Please take a seat gentlemen , we will take your orders " . After much chair shuffling and bringing together of tables we were finally seated and the band , who , having increased the volume during this disturbance receded to normal volume. "Beer everyone" ? The order was placed . Some two beers later , the food and the drink . I was busting for a pee . On inquiry from a waiter he pointed to a door and on walking through it , I entered the urinal , Fifteen by fifteen feet ,with floor channels running into a large drain hole which had two foot plates either side of the hole . At last . Oh ! The relief . It's the little things in life . And . Looking down confirmed the statement . The door opened and in walked a woman , immaculately dressed in an evening gown . Came over to me where I had parked myself for a wee next to the footplate . Greeted me , and then stood on the footplates over the hole , pulled up her dress to her thighs adjusted her underwear and proceeded to wee into the hole . She kept on talking to me and was looking at wee willie so I dropped another finger over him and thought , there , two should be enough to block prying eyes but it didn't stop her trying . She finished, put down her dress , smiled and said to me something which could have been Good night and walked demurely out of the door . I made my way back to the table where the lads were sat and looked around the room but could not see my peeing partner anywhere . "Okay John "somebody asked . I offered a very thoughtful , yes . but said nothing of the experience . These lads must have hollow legs , where are they putting all this beer , I was starting to get dizzy and was grateful when one of the lads suggested going to another place . Outside the air clung to you like a damp cloth . Fortunately the next bar was around the corner and next to it there was a four foot wall on four sides forming an open square room . On my question Reg offered , "it's a toilet" . We entered the bar . Not the same class as the previous but better for atmosphere. I was starting to feel badly due to the drink and remembering the toilet made my way outside to use its facilities . The walls contained , opposite the entrance , a channel some eighteen inches wide and how deep I'm not bothered, the stink was rife . I later found out they used prisoners , as punishment for their crimes , to empty the troughs . I started to pee but felt really sick . It was then I heard someone ,,several , running toward me , their sandals pitta patted on the urinal floor which caused me to turn and saw through blurred eyes three Arabs running towards me. The sudden jerk of my turning made me vomit as I have never vomited before and I sprayed a semi circle of sick toward the running assailants who, because they were wearing flip flop type sandals, I couldnt see theirs but everybody wore them, skidded on the sick and fell onto their backsides and slid past me and into the trough. Someone had seen their intention and had run into the bar to raise the alarm to my crewmates who came bounding out and two of them in their rush, nearly ended up joining the three Arabs in the trough. I remember glancing back at the trough and seeing the three climbing out, their white galabias absolutely covered in excrement . You shouldn't pick on a man who can't defend himself . Because I was in no state to carry on , Reg , good old Reg , hailed a taxi and took me back to queen and country . This ship , set in a silver sea . I vaguely remember the gangway and the rhetorical questions, Right get him below and give him a bucket . " Are you joining us "! ". Wha ' , Coming alive after a night never to be forgot. "Come on John rise and shine or you'll have boson round your neck and we'll all cop it then ". Wha ' ." Oh chuck him in the shower that'll bring him too ". It did . But it didn't make me feel any better . Refusing breakfast I must have sunk four mugs of tea and was about to have a fifth when boson called us all out on deck ." Thank you lads for not causing any problems for me last night . Now why cant you do that all the time . What's up with you John" ? "Oh , something I must have eaten " . Then , oh fuck I I suddenly remembered , my shirts , where were they . I thought , and then thought harder still , and wanted to race down to my room to check but boson continued ." We are pulling out in an hour and were going to La Caruna . Northern Spain .". "Oh , lovely senorita " , "Pete , shut it ! . We'll be dropping our first load of logs there so that will free up the decks . For now just keep yourselves busy and get ready to leave" ."   I raced down to my cabin from the bosons dismissal ,but alas , no shirts until , Reg , stood there , waving the package . "Looking for these ?". "Oh cheers Reg "," Its nothing to do with me . Pete spotted them after we caught the taxi back and brought them back ". Yes ! Perfect . See you on deck . ! I quickly changed into one of the shirts , brilliant , put my fag packet into one of the pockets and buttoned it , yes , now let's see you grab my fags . Then , at the realization of my action ,took the cigarettes back out of the shirt and took off the shirt . How petty . I didn't have to pay for the taxi , they all chipped in . They bought the drinks ,the food , paid for the night club . On deck once more , in my old shirt Bill quipped ." Thought you'd have your new shirt on" . "Nah ! What's a fag or two between crewmates" . They had tested , I had passed . Oh ! . Let's get to Spain. I'm sick and tired of the ship being at a forty five degree angle . The crew were bantering over a cuppa . Were lucky we haven't hit a roller (a heavy sea) No , piped another , the old girl is struggling , we only made two and a half knots yesterday because of the tide , so the mate was saying when I took him the log reading . "Yes , Four more days and we'll be there " .

Chapter 13

"Our grand arrival ". Spain ! , Espania . Another called ". Get the bull ready I'm coming ashore ". "Pete for effin hells sake , you'd be alright facing a bull . You'd have all on facing a senorita" . Guffaws of laughter . Boson "," you can forget about going ashore until all the logs are off deck and you have opened all the hatches . So let's work as a team ", and , to a man we did . By lunchtime the following day the decks were clear and as we were opening the hatches the ship righted itself . Between a hooray from us and a Olay from the dockside we reset the hawser springs and were planning our evening . Was it a sightseeing excursion or a cultural visit to the local museum . Well it was cultural of a kind .. Pub and senoritas of course . A few Olay's ! and we were off on the town . Now keep control , I told myself . Don't let them overload you . Refuse one in three . "C'mon John , them four are yours ". Oh heck , here we go again and tried in vain to catch up . I wouldn't mind but during the evenings binge they had had their oats , every single one of them . Some nice looking girls too . Me , I had to try and fight off a sixty two year old wanting to relive her youth and a woman with three kids , the oldest being about my age . They're calling her mama and she's trying to tell me she's a virgin . What a night . The inevitable happened . I was having trouble knowing what I was doing and my crew mates. They are now trying to chat up this girl to help me launch my career of debauchery . No no she persisted he's too drunk . Naw , he's just shy . I couldnt make her out , what she looked like or anything . She eventually took my arm and half led , half carried me outside . I remember one of the crew pushing some pasetas in my hand and saying , don't pay a penny more . She carried me through the streets and I started becoming aware of us entering a building and climbing some wooden stairs . Walked into a room with an iron bed with a striped mattress . An old woman came in and between their gesturing they eventually gave up and forced my hand open that was gripping the money which the old dear took charge of and exited the room ." Come ", I turned to the voice . The girl now whale like , had obliterated the bed with her girth , naked save for some unusual knickers ? They were like a Persian carpet . It was then I realized it was hair , in fact she was all hair . Not just Pubic hair but hair everywhere . Right , yer bugger , looking through bleary vision , where have yer hidden it . She must have read what I was thinking and with two fingers opened the gateway . I wouldn't say it was frightening but I could have turned to stone there and then . In my drunken state , at her gesture , she indicated for me to free willy . It was like David facing goliath but this time with a very different outcome . Wee willie took one look and tried to get back inside my pants . I dragged him back out but it was no use. He just rolled over and played dead. Even looked through one eye at me to see if he had convinced me.. She got off the bed and mimed I had had too much to drink, At the same time the old lady, madam, came in with a bowl of water whereupon the girl squatted over it and washed herself. Obviously pretending sex had taken place. The old lady poured me a drink and put it to my lips but I pushed it away and headed dizzily back down the stairs and into the street. Somehow I found my way back to the bar but alas. The crew had moved on. I walked, by guesswork through the streets. Having to halt at a doorway for a pee and being confronted by the occupants who, on opening their door, chased me to the end of the street shouting abuse . I eventually saw the dock lights in the distance and took a bearing . Weaving my way through a few more streets I entered the dock gates . There , in front of me . The most beautiful ship , gorgeously painted in baby shh er brown. I was home . I had reasonable control by now but put every effort into boarding and greeted the watch . However , once in my cabin I laid on the bed and the room began to spin . I was ill that night , I vowed never , ever , as God is my witness . Make me better and I'll never do it again. I crawled out of bed in the morning desperate for a cup of tea . The crew were all there and gave an unwelcome cheer . How did it go one enquired ." You set me up good and proper you lot . She was so hairy . It looked like a gorilla with its eyebrows plucked . "They all laughed . "We were just having a laugh" . "Yes , and at my expense "..The following night they carried me back yet again . Sat me on the toilet . Put my head on a pillow and left me there . So much for never drinking , ever again . Next morning I kept a very low profile and just went about my daily chores . Drink proved a problem for me , or at least holding it . I had to come to terms with the fact I was never going to be able to keep up with this lot . So , when the boson announced we were pulling out tomorrow and heading for Bremen to unload the remaining cargo I immediately volunteered for gangway duty to avoid a three in a row outcome . That night , on deck . I looked out on the town , my mind started to drift in thought .

Chapter 14

"Go on , you can do it . What are you waiting for" ? Slowly I began to inch myself along the bowsprit. . The Vindicatrix figurehead was a half naked woman . The bowsprit rope netting had long been removed to deter ratings from the ritual of titting the wooden goddess. I had promised myself, before I left Sharpness to complete this mission. A once in a lifetime experience but now halfway along the carving I was kicking myself but knew it would be the last chance I would have before leaving Sharpness tomorrow morning . "Go on Yorkie ", I gathered up my resilience and moved forward . The sprit was getting awfully narrow . Am I there reaching down ? a bit more forward . Crikey , has she got her tits on her forehead . If this isn't it , I told myself reaching down I'm turning back .. The wooden orbs filled my palms and I didn't know what felt softer . The wooden tits or , Linda Ropers sock filled bra . Back on the deck , bravado overtook nerves , or did it . I managed to say ,"Nothing to it" . It took a while to drop off back in my bunk . Home tomorrow. Oh , bloody hell. That long walk to the station . Goodbye ablutions. Goodbye toilet rolls for shaving cut stoppers . Last breakfast ." Now you go to your pool and register with them" . The officer instructed . All the people who were leaving the training school that day had been called to the office for a final briefing . He continued . "They will give you the train fare home . This ticket is only valid today so don't think you can go tomorrow ". To a man , Yes Sir . "Good luck to you all" . Handshakes all round and off we ventured , out into the world . Back we trudged, baggage in hand . The train station seemed closer and upon arrival , standing on the platform were the four girls from the social village dance . "Where are you four off to" ?. "Were going back to Uni ". Then . "Sorry we couldn't mix with you at the village hall" . "Oh ! That's alright . We understand" . "It's just our parents insist" she went on . "Really it wasn't a problem . We consoled ourselves with your biscuits". the girls laughed ." Yeh ! That will go down in the village register" , more laughter . The arrival of the train ended any structure to be made , bidding farewells we took to the carriages. A guy from Wakefield and myself arrived , late afternoon , at Goole . We left our luggage at the station and headed for the Pool office ." Right young man , your to report here on Monday morning no later than 9.30 . You'll be joining a cargo ship in Falmouth " . "Can't I go direct from Sheffield? ". "No , were sending you with another seaman who has years of experience. It will be better for you and give you an opportunity to discover what it's all about ". Outside the other cadet shook my hand , "you jammy bugger . You've got a ship straight away" . "Yes , Monday" I mused . Today is Friday. Just two days at home .

I walked into my home . My sister gave me a nod and then went into the room . My brother was on his way out and said a quick . Hey ! Bye . Where was the bunting . The band . The crowds singing for he's a jolly good fellow . My popularity diminished I headed for my bedroom. From one iron frame bed to another. What a homecoming this is. "John" my mother's voice called. I ran downstairs to greet her where I was finally met with a hug. How long! Two days. "I've got to report on Monday". Sunday night packing. The nerves were kicking in. Hope I'm doing the right thing. Monday, I bade a nonchalant farewell. Well, that's if anyone bothered listening. Target, Goole pool. On arrival I was introduced to Tony. He had been in the merchant navy eight years. We were both travelling to Falmouth. "I wonder if we are on the same ship", "Could be". First leg, travel down to London. We were in a carriage that filled by the time we got to Doncaster. With the heat in the carriage it was inevitable that I fell asleep. What I didn't know was that I was using the lady next to me as a headrest and was finally awakened by her husband when I wrapped my arms around her and snuggled in. The lady and the carriage occupants were in stitches laughing at my antics as I dragged myself back to consciousness. Completely oblivious to my actions until Tony explained to me whereupon I sincerely apologised to the lady and her husband. So embarrassing. At Kings Cross, the lady wished me well and gave me a quick kiss on my cheek.

Chapter 15

"Thank goodness. The toreadors, making their way back, could be heard streets away. And, what's that? female voices as well. We awaited with trepidation for what they were bringing back to the ship . There . On the dock , .six crew and four lady's of the night . Two of the lads came up the gangway . Wrapped their arms around Reg and myself and tried to walk us away from the gangway . Their intention was to try and sneak the girls past us . Breaking free became a wrestling match and resulted in Alan hitting me accidentally in the face . Staggering back I fell over Reg and Pete who were wrestling on the deck . This was getting totally out of hand and quite frightening when their your own mates ." Stop . Now just stop ." Cor , my lip felt as though it was twice the normal size and I was having difficulty speaking clearly . Who should come on deck . "Everything okay Perkins" . "Its Parkin sir . Yes Sir everything is fine ". "Good , carry on ". I felt like shouting , "Have one for me Sir" but thankfully restrained myself . " Look Alan ". I started to explain . "Is it worth having another months pay docked . Especially if it comes out there's been violence ". The mood of drunken people changes so quickly that I wasn't expecting him suddenly sobbing , embracing me and trying to kiss me better . Oh for fuck sake , can't we go back to fighting . Reg had gone to the bottom of the gangway and informed the rest of the buggers that the second mate was on deck threatening to dock a months pay . The lads , now being reasoned with started to kiss the lady's goodnight . The ladies mood changed dramatically as they demanded loss of earnings . I went down to the quayside to try and help Reg and hustle the crew on board away from the women . Whack , straight across the ear

, a handbag, from one of the lady's for my intervention. They continued screaming abuse as the crew, Reg and I hastily sought sanctuary on deck. The ruckus had brought the boson out of his bunk." What the ! What's happening lads". "The lads were coming aboard " I explained." Those women tried to pick them up. Then they got upset when the lads refused, they started shouting". Lie or not, it sounded convincing and suddenly everyone added agreement to my explanation. The boson, renowned for being the British champion for his bunk said." Good lads. Get to your bunks and keep down the noise ".

" You ok John ", Reg enquired. "Not really", through my swollen lip. "Well, wait a bit then go and get us both a mug of tea". Two hours later. Relieved from duty I crawled into my bunk and sank into a welcome deep sleep . I didn't even hear when we left port ." John ! What have you done to your face "? "Morning boson , I walked into my door last night" . "Yer don't do things by half do you" . I laughed at his comment . Alan was sitting in the canteen and was visibly squirming in his seat ." Well ", boson went on , "Get your breakfast and come on deck , you too Alan ". When he had gone Alan offered , "John , I'm really sorry for punching you last night . I must have been absolutely pissed out of my mind ". "Yep , you were ". I left the canteen and made my way forward . "Ah , just the man . Crikey , what happened to you" ? . "Morning to you too Chief engineer . Would you believe it if I said I walked into a door" ? "No ". "Then I will not lie to you . How can I help sir ". "Well . It's the second engineers birthdays today . He's on duty at the moment so could you fasten this banner I've made to the second deck. "."I can . But . Have you checked with the boson "?Oh , don't worry . It should be ok " . He left me with the banner . Hmm ! There's something fishy going on here ." Got a minute boson " ," Hi John , what's up ! . Hmm , that's odd . Yer did right to come to me . Let's have a look what's written on the banner . It's in French I think . Nah John , doesn't sound right leave it with me . I'll ask if someone speaks French" . No sooner had I got back down aft ." Quick John , put it up" . "What's it say boson". " The second engineer invites everyone to his birthday . Free beer for all . So quick . He'll be up in a minute " . We were putting the last knot on the banner when his feet hit the deck . HAPPY BIRTHDAY to you rang out and he looked up . "Which @#$%*$#@#$ has @$#%$@#&%$ put that up" . The chief engineer shouted . "John's done it ". The rest of the crew wholeheartedly supported the chief engineer . Charlie , the chief steward , being in on the ruse flung the pantry doors open and four cases of lager were deposited on No 3 hatch complete with bottle openers . For he's a jolly good fellow soon gave way to everyone drinking the cool nectar . I managed to give reassurance to the second engineer . "I don't speak French ." " I know whose responsible son . It'll be his turn next month ". Twelve bottles to a case times four cases supped . "More" came the pleas . "Where do they put it ? ! Yeh ! Go on then". Eight more cases later the second engineer called it enough, much to the relief of Charlie seeing his only food source dwindling. I wonder if he's put a beer stache in the lifeboats. At last, nobody was interested in tea and coffee. That night we were passed by a Royal navy frigate. They decided to show their skill on the Aldiss lamp. The speed they achieve is unbelievable. We had a handheld torch and a Morse code handbook. I can only assume that half the frigates company died of laughter that night as we tried to reply. It's a wonder they didn't board us for suspected piracy. Days later we were hailed by the white cliffs. There's something about those shores. This demi paradise. Of course, William Shakespeare. Who else.

Chapter 16

On , up the North sea , into the Weser passing Bremerhaven and through the locks to Bremen . Our final dumping ground for these blessed logs . Possibly , one of the dirtiest cargos ever in terms of disposal of residue. I had , for some time even before joining the ship , had an urge to buy a guitar . I approached the boson to arrange an advance against my wages . Informing him what it was for . "What ! A guitar ! Where are you going to play it . You can't disturb the lads "." I'll go on the boat deck . Nobody can hear me up there ". "Are you sure you want to waste your money on a guitar ". "Well , so far I've wasted it on booze and I've got nothing to show for it "." Ok ! Leave it with me ". " A guitar" ! The first mate said handing me the cash . "Can you play ?. Whose going to teach you ? . Have you thought about it "? . Crikey , I thought to myself . If it was booze fags and women they wouldn't bat an eyelid . "I think the way things are going it may be the only thing I have to show that I've actually earned something sir .".A smile and a shake of the head he warned . "Don't go disturbing the lads off duty" . Thanking him I returned to my cabin . The boson had given me the day off . I boarded a tram near the docks to take me to the town . The conductor, fortunately for me spoke English. I said I was looking for a guitar shop . He suddenly rang the tram bell , stopping the vehicle ,and beckoned me to the tram footplate where he pointed to a shop . Its windows bursting with guitars . Thanking him I crossed the street and after briefly looking at the window display I entered the shop where I was approached by a smiling elderly man .who greeted me in German . His face grimaced when I returned his greeting but in English . He abruptly returned to his office and spoke rather loudly , and very angrily to a secretary who after minutes of chatter came and greeted me in English . My first words to her was . "Have I upset him" . "He's old ". She replied . "I'm wanting to buy a guitar ". She took me to some wall cabinets holding the most beautiful guitars I had ever seen before or since . Asked me my budget. Closed the cabinet and guided me toward a cheap , by comparison , selection of guitars . I should have left there and then in hindsight but , young and daft was my demeanour walking out several minutes later cradling a guitar .

Now, how do I get back to the ship. Everything looked different. Crossing the road I scanned the docks in the distance. There she was. Baby shit beige but home. About a hundred yards to where she was berthed I noticed a river ferry leaving its berth and plying it's way across and near to my location. But how do I get down there. There were some workmen unloading a lorry, I approached them. "Excuse a da me. How get to river ferry ". Why do we think if we speak in broken English that they will understand. They ignored me. Again, excuse me can you. "Go !" said one of the loaders, a severe looking fellow. One of the others with him said something, which prompted him to continue ". Nien" Italiano ". So he thinks I'm Italian. "No. Me English". Which just made matters worse. He started growling and becoming more aggressive . One of the loaders was a lad , roughly my age . He jumped down and beckoned me to follow and subsequently pointed the way down to the ferry . I was glad when I finally set foot on the gangway of our ship . This piece of England , berthed in a foreign land . No sooner than I I had walked into the mess the guitar was taken out of my hands by Pete . "You got it then" ."Yes , Er , be careful". My concern falling on deaf ears save for the strumming of the guitar . "Here Pete , let's have a go" . Alan grabbed the guitar and attempted to play it . Twang ! . Top E snapped . Roars of laughter , but not from me . "Take it back John , it's no good " wasn't quite the encouragement I wanted to hear so I offered "Here , let me fix it for you "and removed the broken string ." I'll leave it on the table so you can have a play with it " and with that, dejectedly, I went up on deck. The following day, much to my surprise, Alan pushed two sets of strings in my hand but, I never really played the guitar much after that day ." C' mon, get ready we're going ashore tonight " was all we needed to break the monotony of being trapped in port. Strange, you miss the motion and the freedom after just a few days. That night, the taxi dropped us off at " The Golden City " Pete announced. We entered the establishment, I don't really know what you could call it, it was like a concert hall but the tables were set on four sides of the room .A bit like a medieval banqueting room. Pete having been before on a previous trip spoke to a waiter who sat us down on the far side of the room . Beers all round I looked around the room . The tables at the top of the room were occupied by some very beautiful women , elegantly dressed. The tables directly from them at the bottom of the room were seated the roughest women I had ever seen . Amongst them were men , dressed in women's clothing . I couldnt work out what looked the most revolting , the men or the old lady's. Directly across from us the girls were very smart . But lacking the elegance of the top tables . So our tables were third rate . But I was glad we wasn't sat amongst the dock rats of the cheap tables . Two girls pushed their way in between our group . One , a young blonde woman grabbing my groin , " Fucky fucky Johnnie" . Having spent most of my money on the guitar I enquired "How much ", then a typical

Yorkshireman reply of "How much " astounded by the cost of a two minute tribute to the Father Christmas syndrome. " Get in , empty your sack , and then get back out ". My comment ." No , I'm fine" saw the two move to more victims . I became aware of something or some presence around me . My gaze was drawn to the top table where , on searching the faces , my eyes rested on a very beautiful girl looking straight at me who 's smile sent a surge of need through my very being . I didn't have the money but upon her beckoning , I rose from my chair to join her . I didn't return to the ship that night with the others . In my life , as we all have been at one time or another , I was used , but this will always remain , the most pleasantly memorable used . So that's what it's all about . I felt ten feet tall the following morning. Absolutely fantastic. Skint , who cares about money . Magda ordered a taxi for me and gave the driver instruction plus the fare . On arrival at the ship I walked up that gangplank on air , my dream disturbed by reality " Where do you think you've been " . With a stupid grin on my face I replied "Heaven " the word frozen on my lips as I realized the enquirer was the second mate . "Well I hope you think it was worth it because the Mate is docking your pay . Now get aft and get some work done , the canteen is a tip " . They could have docked a years pay . It was only when I started calculating my wages one night that I had spent almost as much as I had earned what with the fines and all . Was this working ? . Yes , of course it was . No traffic to contend with , no clocking in and out , no waiting for buses , no bells or whistles telling me it's time for a cuppa or to go to a home . Well , that's not strictly true. We have a bell . But four hours in twelve save for the dog watches is my kind of shift . I didn't go ashore that night , instead , volunteered . Watch duty . "Feeling hungry son "? "Oh , sorry Captain , er ! Yes Sir, I am a bit hungry " . " Just outside the dock gates " he went on "at the end of the road there's a shop selling frankfurters " . Hmm , never had one of those before . "Get six of the largest , their about two foot long ," stuffing cash into my hand he added "Quick as you can " . Upon reaching the instructed destination it was just like a chip shop back home , same type of frying pans but the sausages were taken straight from the pan to the bread roll . My turn . Still could not speak any German but my miming skills had improved vastly . Held six fingers up and then indicated length by open hands , just hoping she didn't think I was bragging . Back on board ship . "Come in " . answered my requested knock on the Captains door . "Ah! Good lad just the job " . The cabin looked like an office . There were rooms leading off , A large desk occupied the centre of the room with four leather bound chairs paying it homage in which sat the first and second mate and the second engineer . Behind the desk sat the Captain , his high back chair reminded me of a picture I once saw at school of king Canute turning back the waves . They were joined by the Chief engineer entering the room " Oh hello John , how you doing ". The five were obviously in deep discussions and as I handed out the frankfurters the first mate was saying U.S. that's probably the best option . " Have the last one for yourself son " took me by complete surprise, then . " Could you knock us up a cup of tea ". " Make mine a coffee no sugar .tea one sugar no milk " . "How many for coffee , how many for tea and I'll bring the sugar and milk separately so you can put in your own ", I couldn't believe I had spoken to the top brass of the ship with such authority and awaited a condemning rebuke, instead , "Good idea" . As I got to the door ,"Here , don't go without your frankfurter ". Whilst waiting for the kettle to boil in the amidships galley , I ravenously devoured the frankfurter . Who should come staggering in . Our Charlie . "What are you up to lad " . I explained . " We have stewards for that . Nip down and ask Jeff to come and see me " . " Hes gone ashore chief " . "Oh , well can you make it then "and turned and headed back to his room and his beer . Poor sod . Drinks delivered . Back on deck I joined Alan who I was on duty with . " Everything ok ! " answering "Yes" to his enquiry . "Do you fancy a drink of tea Alan " . I hadn't spoken much to him since the fight even less since breaking the guitar string . It broke the ice and the tension between us and the remainder of the shift was spent in friendly banter . The following morning the second mate entered the aft mess room along with the boson whilst we were having breakfast . "I suppose you're all aware by now where our next trip is " and looked at me directly. I had not said anything that I had overheard in the Captain's room. Upon realizing this from the crews response, his attitude toward me changed from that day. "We are off to the United states. Florida ". Excitedly the crew exchanged expressions, some good some bad. Were picking up a cargo at Belgium so I want you all to clean the holds from top to bottom, "Okay ! Right get to it ". Absolute chaos ensued as we just could not resist, accidentally of course, spraying the boson who had come to check on our progress. Retaliation? Why most definitely. It became farcical. So much so that we found ourselves standing in two feet of salt water when the boson eventually called a halt to the proceedings. Sodden to the bone we squelched out of the hold

.Two days later we had it dried out and was looking forward to our shore leave in Belgium. That night , retiring to my bunk . What a great job this is and my thoughts took me back .

Chapter 17
Kings Cross underground. We had to make our way across London to Paddington station . When there , our Enquirer informed us "The train to Penzance doesn't leave until nine thirty PM. Change at Truro . Three hours to kill in the most expensive city in England . We handed our kit in to the left luggage and decided at Tony's suggestion to try and find the seafarers mission . He explained it was a place where we could get cheap drinks and something to eat . Even have a game of table tennis or

snooker. He took the lead, asking several people for directions and after a walk of about three miles we arrived at a long building with steps leading to a single wooden door. "Are you sure this is the place" my uncertainty only made his reply more expletive. "Yes, this is it let's go and get something to eat and play a game. His second wrap upon the door knocker brought forth a woman of about twenty five. It was then I noticed above the door there was a red light and as Tony was trying to tell the lady. "We've come for a bite q to eat and a game of " I thought to myself. It's not going to be table tennis in here tonight and grabbing his arm I apologized to the woman for disturbing her customary performance. When I pointed out the red light to Tony he still insisted this was the bloody seaman's mission . "For goodness sakes Tony . Let's get back to the station ". Grumbling, he lamented . " Well it used to be a seamen's mission once ". And I offered . "To some , it still is " . We trudged back to Paddington railway station . At last . Good old Great Western . We boarded the delayed train at ten thirty . "Sorry for the delay gents "the guard of the train had been instructed to offer disgruntled passengers .We quickly found an empty carriage and using my overcoat as a blanket I quickly joined in as Bass to Tony's Tenor . Snoring . Neither one of us , admitted later , to budging an inch . It was only when Tony , disturbed by the guards request . "Tickets gentlemen " . " John , the guard wants your ticket " . Then more forcedly. "John " . Sleepily I replied " Its up there on the shelf " to which, both Tony and the guard burst out laughing, bringing me into semi consciousness. Searching my overcoat pockets, I produced the ticket. He bade us good morning informing us that we would arrive at Truro in fifteen minutes. This was the wake up call we needed and hurriedly retrieved our kit from the luggage rack. The train ground to a halt. Stepping down out of the train onto the station the verification from the station guard calling " Truro, Truro station ". We enquired from him our connection to Falmouth. " The little train over there gents " leaves in ten minutes ". Just enough time to grab a bite to eat from the station canteen. Half starved I chose the biggest pasty they had and scoffing it it greedily, headed for the connection train. Talk about the Titfield

Thunderbolt , it was ancient . Something out of a museum . We climbed into the wooden carriage, no corridor , something from another era of decayed granduer and settled down for our final ride to our destined floating home . The train finally set off and we quickly noticed the smoke from the engine was becoming increasingly toxic. We tried to close the carriage door windows but both belts to raise the windows had long since rotted and broken . Coughing and spluttering we eventually reached Falmouth station . Well ,on arrival , we looked like Rastus and Remus from the black and white minstrels . A taxi had been sent by the Falmouth Pool office to collect us .When the driver eventually stopped laughing he offered " I'll take you to a wash place before we go to the pool office " . Recleansed , we entered the Pool office . "Your all going to need your jabs " the guy behind the counter Informed us , and we were transferred by taxi to the doctors . Five people on one needle no wonder the last two cried out ,and then onward to the dock and , our ship .

Chapter 18
" John , its six o clock " . " Ok Alan , thanks " . Out on deck the air had a chill but a very bright morning . We could now make out through the haze the Belgian coastline and an hour later entering the jaws of the waterway that takes us to arguably the largest lock system in the world , save for counting Panama . The locks of Antwerp . Adolf Hitler's brilliant but fated Battle of the bulge to capture

Antwerp docks and sue for a ceasefire to end the war . However . Llike Napoleon before him . Failed in his attempt. The tugs nudged us into position and the laying of the hawsers and springs went like a charm . Later that evening , we who were on lookout called the second mate to the deck as the wind speed had increased and asked should we double the lines . His "No, it will be alright " cost us two weeks in dry dock when we broke free at two in the morning . One thing I will say . That's the last decision he made . His replacement joined us a week later . A man of about fifty or so . Alan and Pete had their heads together and tried it on , calling him number two but the guy was too experienced and by docking them a weeks pay brought them and any other smart arse to heel . Repairs done and finally fully loaded , we set sail for America. Again passing Dover and along the Seven Sisters .So close to home and then In to what seemed an unending ocean . Our speed of two and a half knots , now ,blatantly surpassed thanks to some of the work carried out in dry dock increased to three and a half knots . It still took us two and a half weeks to cross the Atlantic . When you think that the Cunard Queens , Elizabeth and Mary were doing the crossing in three to four days or so , just no comparison . We received an emergency weather report when we were a hundred miles from the Florida coastline . We were heading into a hurricane . That afternoon we were passed by a US cargo ship .Then . That night , we ran into the storm . How quickly the sea can change . We were lucky as our slowness put us behind the main force of the storm . Sadly the US cargo ship that had passed us , we later found out ,was broken in two with a loss of all hands . We eventually sighted land and thanks to modern technology we were just thirty miles off course and tramped down the coast to Fort Lauderdale . Docked . The storm had left a foot of sand on the dock and road . The crew had been talking about Wrangler industrial Jean's being hard wearing . I was given the task of making a list of size per person and loaded with money was given the afternoon to shop for the crew . Your in a strange country and you think it's the same as England . That is until you try and use their facilities, or bus services , or their livestock and then you get a rude awakening. Mine was in the form of a sidewinder snake racing across my pathway, missing me by inches . My second was in town crossing the road . We look right and left then right . But , we look for traffic on the left hand side of the road . So stepping off a pavement a disgruntled driver got the opportunity to use his Christmas box , pressing the damned horn for what seemed an eternity . I returned his greeting which seemed to upset him more ." Makes you proud to be British "! . At last after what seemed a re enactment of Scott's quest for the South Pole a shop emblazoned "Wotkwear Industrials " .

Chapter 19
 Stepping inside a helpful young guy approached , Upon him realizing that I

was English , he was full of questions and for half an hour we chatted on . He was a student , working something or other , I cant recall which year study he was in . His boss eventually came across to put an end to the discussion but upon hearing I was English his eyes widened . He had been stationed in Britain during the war in supplies and later , in the closing stages , had transferred to Antwerp . "We have just come from Antwerp " . Set him off reminiscing once more . Eventually . "How can we help you ?" . Explaining, I produced the list . "Levi , nothing compares with Levi " . This shopkeeper , with twenty plus years of experience had the list completed in ten minutes . "Where are you berthed ?". Oh heck . I had forgotten to notice so quickly recalled and described the port surroundings. He turned to the student who I now know as Harry, explained to him the location of the ship and told him to get the truck from out back whilst we settle the bill." If ever your in " followed by an enthusiastic hand shake that took a while for the blood to become recirculated, he waved me goodbye. Harry was chatting and said he and a couple of his mates were going to see a film that night. "Ben who "?. "Hur. Charlton's Heston. Have you not heard. Its supposed to be a real blockbuster". I had no knowledge about the film but Harry's enthusiasm and his offer to "Swing by the ship at six thirty ish " was an offer I could not refuse. At last people my age but poles apart I found out later, in culture. That evening on the dot, six youths, crammed into the back of the truck with three girls up front with Harry driving . With much honking and screaming . "C'mon John " , I was yanked into the back of the truck and we must have lost an inch of tread with the tyres smoking till they finally found purchase . Not the comfortable ride enjoyed earlier . Trying to understand the conversation proved impossible. We skidded to a halt outside a coffee shop ,, the curb thankfully acting as a failsafe . Tera firma , you never felt more welcoming . The cinema directly opposite was our target but first intros . "This is " . By the third I had forgotten the first . The girls wanted to go into the drinks bar for a coke and we said no way ,the film comes first second and third . . So after the coke we crossed and entered the cinema . The noise from the banter finally , was brought to a close by the cinema lights dimming . My ears welcoming the sanctified rest from the chatter which I confess , just didn't understand . What a film . The chariot race . Genius ! . Captured by the thrill of the chase I suddenly had an awful thought . We have to go back in Harry's employers truck . Harry was revved to breaking relating the final laps of the chariot race and I noticed his manner in relating the enactment was transferred to the truck drive back to the ship . The girls screaming on every corner taken , the lads solemnly quiet save for a few whimpers , did their best not to join in with the girls . Alighting from the chariot oops , truck , I couldn't help saying , "Our Father" and bade the truck and its occupants "Safe Journey " . "Thanks for a great evening ". It was later, I was reflecting on the evening and began to realise we don't really have that much in common with each other. The following evening I went for a walk around the town. I had decided to wear my suit, grey and black stripes. A policeman mounted on a Harley Davidson motorcycle pulled up along side me and turned up the volume of his radio broadcasting, " White Male, striped suit short curly hair, wanted for raping a black girl. Her family are out looking for the youth. The policeman nodded good evening and pulled away on his motorcycle. Penny dropped, with a clatter of a manhole cover. Although totally innocent ? He had assumed that I was the culprit and instead of questioning me had warned me to get off the street. I hailed a taxi and headed back to the ship . The Levi Jean's I had brought back the previous day were first scorned by the crew but on second inspection found they were so tough we had to run a bath tub of water to try and soften the material . Later on the third day of soaking . We tried them out . It was like hobbling around with two planks down your trouser legs . More soaking and eventually they became almost wearable . My pair were finally given full burial honours some eighteen years later . Best value for money ever and with their demise the ghost of a frightening truck drive finally laid to rest .

Chapter 20

Next port of call , Tampa . The Everglades opposite our berth looked foreboding . Could never understand . The rain for three days fell not more than forty feet away upon the Everglades but never on us. Strange phenomenon. Some of the dock lads had been talking to Pete about a bar we must visit, supposedly all action. Don't exactly know what action they are used to but when we got there it was full but just a mumbling. No music, no jukebox, just, mumbling. The room was about forty foot long by eighteen feet so quite narrow. Bar on one side facing a long bench seat which ran almost the length of the room. After a couple of drinks I needed the loo. Locking the door which faced the whole length of the bench. Someone tried the door." I wont be a minute " should have sufficed but no. The door was ripped open ,Security bolt flying off to anywhere, and a whole bench full of people watching me taking a leak . Calmly , no murderous intention ," Cheers Pete , could you close the door please ". "No I cant wait " and joined me in synchronized peeing , surely a first for a shit tip bar in Tampa and , an audience who didn't even have the good manners to clap ." Weve been kicked out of places better than this ", was the last thing I heard Pete saying to the bar man . "Where to now ", the night was still young . We hadn't passed anything so let's keep walking . I noticed a clearing on the other side of a stream . It was boarded off all around the perimeter and approximately three feet high. Inside the clearing were young Christmas trees. I got an idea that as it was Christmas in three weeks I would come back tomorrow with an axe . Further along the track I heard music . "Great , look at this place " . Country music blaring . A hoot and a hollering . We entered . The bar man treated us like royalty . Organised a table and kept the beer flowing . For some strange reason , I never got drunk . So this revelation was a greater phenomenon than the rain on the Everglades. I must have drunk eight beers , usually out for the count on three or four , didn't feel anything . I turned to Pete "Hey Pete , Pete "? . Lying on the floor . He'd slipped out of the chair Pissed as a fart . We were two miles easily from the ship . "What are we gonna do with him " . "We'll carry him " . It was dark now and outside the cricket chorus were tuned to perfection , their sound almost deafening in the thick evening air . "Snakes , What about snakes , And Alligators "" some bright spark offered .

Off we trudged with our Shiralee, a name I learned later visiting Australia, meaning burden. To any observer we must have looked ridiculous, a lump of wood in one hand to beat off alligators and a leg under the other arm. By luck more than judgement we arrived at the ship absolutely ringing in sweat. But safe. "Who's going to carry him down the companionway?. Alan stepped forward. " Here, give him to me ", he put Pete over his shoulder and started down. Now you can only do this for three or four steps, then, the carried persons head starts to make contact with the steps. I think I counted six bumps in all thinking, "His head in the morning is going to hurt something awful ". Following morning I yawned my way into the mess for breakfast. Who should be there, full of

Beans, Pete. "Morning John. After a few chosen expletives not believing what I was witnessing I managed "How do you feel"?. "Fine, couldnt be better "." Have you washed "looking at the black Mark's on his forehead, " I think you ought to go and wash". More of an order than a politely observed suggestion. When he came back from ablutions he said "It will not come off. "." No you burke it's a bruise . Then. "Do you want to come with me to get a Christmas tree " , and went into great detail with my plan . Operation CT , That afternoon we made our way to the fenced area I had noticed the night before. " Why the boards ? surely people can step over .. cmon ". I noticed a really nice tree and decided. This is the one . A few whacks with the fire axe, rattle rattle . "What's that ".

Another whack, rattle rattle rattle. "OH FUCK! Rattlesnakes. We had entered a compound for the collection of venom. We grabbed the felled tree and ran like the wind leaping over the boarded fence, leapt over the stream and although ridiculous, didn't stop running until we sighted the ship. Ridiculous. If the snakes were trapped by the fence, how could they follow?. Frightening experience, lesson learned, we nonchalantly walked the rest of the way at a relaxed gait and met Alan who was coming to find us. The dock workers had rigged an access to the ship bridging a fifteen foot gap between the dock and the ship. However. The end of the bridge although solid on the dockside wasn't quite touching the ship. Three people and a Christmas tree crossing the bridge caused the bridge to counterbalance . Do you run forward or do you run back towards the dock . I was carrying the axe and threw it onto the deck of the ship and as the bridge now at some forty five degrees tilt , I jumped up for the handrail of the ship ,grabbed it , and vaulted over the handrail and onto the deck . Now the pendulum of the bridge was lighter on the ship side and heavier once more on the dockside it reset itself with a teeth shuddering SMACK throwing Alan and Pete a good two feet in the air . It was so funny seeing the fright in there eyes , I shouldn't have laughed really . But I did . And on , and on . Tears now rolling down my face with laughter at their predicament , so funny . Retaliation. Absolutely , nothing would stop the duo from taking revenge . "Fucking Christmas tree " ." You nearly got me killed ". Pete related the rattlesnake experience to the crew . "They collect venom from the snakes for medical reasons " the boson offered . "Never again , and you can stop laughing you little bugger " . " No I cant " more tears . A few years later on reminiscing the incident always made me smile , finally the memory as with the smile , fading with age . The first mate sent for Pete and myself . "What's this about a Christmas tree, who said you could bring it aboard , don't you realize you've committed an offence " . "We , well , I , wanted to bring a little bit of Christmas to the ship " . "We do the organising if there is any organising to be done not you ". Then , "So where is the tree now " . " In the aft kitchen Sir " . "Keep it down there until we sail and then bring it up to the saloon . We'll put it in something , Now bugger off the pair of you and don't do it again ". Two days later we sailed round to Beaumont , Texas , and were loaded with Saltpetre a highly volatile powder . No smoking anywhere except extreme aft and set sail , for Blighty hoorah .

Chapter 21

Two days out from Beaumont , evening time , there were four of us on the boat deck , putting the world to rights when we experienced a strange thing I have no explanation to offer . We had sailed into a cloud resting on the water . We were just commenting on this peculiarity when we noticed, in the cloud an old ships lantern , lit ,Some twenty feet from us passing along our beam ..When it had passed the cloud slowly lifted . All four of us saw this

, apparition , Not one of us had had any drink . " Did you see that " Reg inquired . " What was it , it looked like a lantern , you know , the ones they had on galleon's . "That's what I saw " . "And me" . The sky now darkening but clear plus the chill of our experience with the lantern still on our minds , we turned in, to be ready for the four while eight . Florida had hidden the advance of winter but it soon came upon us when we took the north circle route . Nine days out . The sea had been building into a cauldron of destruction all day . We had rigged rat lines for our safety on deck and had gotten soaking wet through doing it . But that same night it became a monster of a sea . The waves that were coming over onto the deck were some sixty feet . We had to be called on deck to re tie canvas over the deck vents to stop seawater flooding onto the cargo because the mechanism with age had rusted and had been painted and repainted long ago so this was the only alternative . Two were secured successfully but we were being battered by the sea and retrieved our position sheltering on the Lee of the superstructure , away from the full force of the waves coming over the deck , but still underwater at times . During the afternoon , although we had got drenched , putting rat lines in place which was a bit of a laugh . What we were facing now was different all together . The wind was screaming , literally screaming . It was as if every soul lost at sea was screaming " Find me , Find me" making the hairs on the back of my neck stand on end. "Come on lads, just two more and we can get out of this bloody weather. We had one hand on the rat line trying to place the canvas over the intake but were being hampered as the waves crashing on the deck kept putting us under water for what seemed an age. The rat line gave way. Tumbling down the deck underwater I hit something and grabbed hold of it but the power of the sea pushed me bodily through a gap of no more than seven inches between a cabin air intake and a bulkhead. My foot then my leg went through a gunwale anchoring me to the ship. Strangely I felt warm and relaxed and everything was quiet, then, suddenly the screaming was back and I was able to breathe again and gasped at the air to fill my depleted lungs but the rest of me was still underwater . I freed my leg , blind panic kicked in and I waded over to the Lee side being pushed by another wave and took refuge behind the superstructure . Shook up and very frightened . Alan and Pete came around the end of the superstructure to join me . Shaken but seemed in control ." Fucking hell's bells , that was a big fucker" . Relating to the wave . "WHERE'S REG " . Shock became concern and shock . We frantically looked around the deck as best we could constantly being battered by the waves of water , both fore and aft , we checked everything. Accommodation , ablutions Pete ,not hesitating , struggled up the companions leading to the bridge to report the loss . Six short blasts followed by a long blast . Waste of time . We were on deck getting battered by the sea and could hardly hear the ships fog horn due to the screaming of the wind . What can you do in this weather ? What can you do ? If you try to turn you'll lose the ship and everyone on board . You cant stop , same grisly end . In that storm and icy sea you would be dead in six minutes . Then , back in the safety of the aft accommodation Pete' was upset and ranting " Fuck the cargo I'm not going out in that again " . And to a man we all agreed . Thankfully Neil reminded us " Would you go back out to save the ship or rather go down with her . . A few tears were cried that night from us all . Back in my cabin I then remembered of my being knocked through the gap and stripped off to check my body . There wasn't a scratch on me . Impossible through that gap . But the power of the sea made it possible . The storm eventually started to ease at around eleven the following day .That evening the captain held a service on deck and again more tears flowed freely .Sadly coming to terms with the loss of a much respected mate . Our time over the remainder of the trip was difficult for us all . One of the lifeboats had been smashed from its cradles during the storm . A steel door leading down to the holds had been severely buckled . Several port hole glasses on the starboard side had been cracked . The Christmas tree was dumped overboard , no longer a symbol of Merry Christmas .The Christmas dinner , partly eaten then dumped . Statements from us all who were on deck , recollecting that nightmare of a night . Boson's input " Not many people get the chance to die doing the thing they love the most . Rotting in a bed wasn't Reg's idea of life .

Chapter 22

The Seven sister's bowed their heads as we passed and then , the white cliffs of Dover . A few days later we stood at anchor awaiting our pilot and then tug boats to take us into Middlesbrough . We were ready for home but were asked to stay with the ship another week to take her (The ship) down to Immingham . We went out a couple of nights whilst in Middlesbrough but it wasn't the same anymore . Pete was the first to be realistic . " We need to be away from each other" ." It's always going to be with us and if we stay together its all we will ever talk about ". Immingham , There had been an awkward silence amongst us coming down from Middlesbrough" . I think it was because we all knew we had shared great times and yet times of extreme sorrow and most of all the parting of the ways with Reg .The day of farewells . For the past nine months these people have been your family . You will never see them again . I thought to myself. "Just another ten days and we would have celebrated my sixteenth birthday . We had received our pay and surprisingly the fines which had been imposed were not enforced. We had all received full pay . Handshakes abound . I stood on the dockside and took a last look at this babyshit beige tub of a ship . Turning away to control a tear . I climbed into the taxi transferring me to Hull railway station. The clickety click of the train wheels carrying me closer, to what? Finally. Smoky old Sheffield and a bus ride home. Why didn't I get a taxi. Once a pauper etc. Walking into my parents home I was pinned in a vice like hug from my mother which I gladly returned. Then a nod from my brother and finally from my sister. "Oh your back " to which she walked straight past me and out of the door. My family had never earned a lot of money and had been used to getting by on a collective total of eight pounds a week for food and rent. So I made the biggest mistake of my life giving my mother Fifty pounds. A screaming fortune to our type of folk in those days. The following morning I decided to visit my best mates house and found not only him but also four more of my old classmates there all chattering on . I tried to be happy to see them, telling them I had missed their companionship. But things were different, They were still children. These people who I had grown up with all my life were suddenly complete strangers and to my mind, still not ready for the outside world. They invited me to go to the cinema that evening but I made an excuse about having to visit a relative, a complete lie. That afternoon, when I returned home my mother and sister had been shopping. Five dresses each, new shoes, handbag. The money I had given for settling outstanding debts and for food, they had blown the lot. I just stared at them in disbelief. I went to my bedroom to sulk in silence. Not such a grown up after all. This was on the Saturday. I hadn't been at home twenty four hours .On the Monday nine thirty sharp , I made a call to Goole pool . " Can you get me on the first ship available I have got accommodation problems " . Their response was of a cargo ship sailing from Goole first thing Tuesday morning for Copenhagen, "But you would have to sign on before five o clock today ." I'll be there ". I collected together my gear from my parents home .looked around at the place I had accepted as home but now , as foreign as the lands I had left behind . Wrote a note saying I had to report back as it was an emergency . I lied . Slipped out of the house . Into a new adventure. A new family of shipmates .

Printed in Great Britain
by Amazon